JACKSONVILLE

*Center for Enterprise Excellence
on Florida's First Coast*

JACKSONVILLE

Center for Enterprise Excellence
on Florida's First Coast

TEXT BY JANE TANNER
PHOTOGRAPHY BY DIANE UHLEY

LONGSTREET PRESS
Atlanta, Georgia

PUBLISHED IN COOPERATION WITH THE JACKSONVILLE CHAMBER OF COMMERCE

Published by LONGSTREET PRESS, INC.,
a subsidiary of Cox Newspapers,
a division of Cox Enterprises, Inc.
2140 Newmarket Parkway, Suite 118
Marietta, Georgia 30067

Printed in the United States of America

1st printing, 1993

ISBN: 1-56352-122-9

This book was printed by Arcata Graphics, Kingsport, Tennessee.
The text was set in Gilde.

Cover/jacket design by Jill Dible.
Book design by Laurie Shock.

CONTENTS

Foreword

To the people who live and work on Florida's First Coast, it is the best of all possible worlds. The weather is temperate, the lifestyle is comfortable, the economy is diverse enough to resist fluctuations and the work ethic is alive and well.

Jacksonville is proud to be recognized as Florida's business city, a community with a strong history based in commerce and a future that is rich with potential for continued growth and prosperity. Jacksonville offers a climate that is conducive to good business, and leadership which recognizes the value of an encouraging business environment.

The pursuit of economic growth is carefully balanced against the costs of becoming a "big city." The five-county First Coast area — Baker, Clay, Duval, Nassau and St. Johns counties — enjoys a quality of life difficult to duplicate elsewhere. Some newcomers to the area remark that living here makes vacation planning difficult: there are myriad opportunities to enjoy so many things. It's true. When work is done, there are the beaches, dozens of recreational choices for sports enthusiasts and spectators alike, music, festivals, entertainment and plenty of traditional Southern hospitality.

The future of the First Coast is promising and exciting. Community leaders are anxious for reasoned and balanced growth without sacrificing the tangible and intangible elements which make the area attractive. The Jacksonville Chamber of Commerce is proud to be a partner in this effort.

Since its founding in 1884, the Chamber has worked to promote Jacksonville and the business interests of the area. Thousands of volunteers work to facilitate business recruitment, economic development, enhancing the quality of life and contributing to the positive image of Jacksonville. The people and companies located in Jacksonville and the First Coast area care about their community and are committed to making it one of America's finest.

We welcome you to the First Coast area and invite you to play a role in the future of the community we call home.

The Jacksonville Chamber of Commerce

Introduction

Jacksonville, Florida's largest city, defies simple descriptions. To best capture the sense of the city, you have to accept that it has many personalities and immense contrasts. On the one hand, it's a slow, Southern city with a deep blue-collar tradition and a provincial attitude. Yet, Jacksonville is also a fast-paced bustling business community that has grown quickly in the past two decades by expanding local firms and drawing new companies. Just consider that twelve of Florida's 100 largest public companies and 15 of the biggest private firms in terms of revenues are headquartered here.

Drive along the small bridges that cross the patchwork of waterways that are at the heart of Jacksonville — most days you're likely to find a gaggle of fisherman, leisurely basking in the sun, patiently watching the ends of their lines for drum, flounder or croaker to bite. But in that same scene, it's not uncommon to see a huge cargo ship or freighter pass by, hauling cars, coffee and chemicals to and from destinations around the world.

A city where agricultural fairs and mud-truck pulls draw a big crowd, Jacksonville is also host to world-class sporting events such as the PGA Tour Players Championship and the Bausch & Lomb Tennis Championship, featuring the world's top ranked female players. In fact, the international headquarters of the PGA Tour and Association of Tennis Professionals are here in northern St. Johns County.

It is a region of compelling contrasts between small-town culture and big-city characteristics, and the people who live here love having both alternatives. For example, although residents of Northeast Florida claim some of the finest restaurants to be found in the country, the well-heeled here are just as likely to patronize the sampling of fish camps on creeks and inlets where a dinner of all-you-can-eat catfish goes for $8.95.

While Miami and other Florida cities are its brethren, Jacksonville has a greater attachment to South Georgia and Alabama, a researcher of the area once observed.

It's neither a crowded, highly commercial tourist mecca, nor a haven for retirees like other parts of Florida. And it's too far north to be considered tropical. The seasonal changes are milder. People choose to live here because the beaches are quieter, not lined with high-rise condos. Jacksonville is more a stable, livable city with an immense and often pristine natural landscape that includes the St. Johns River, Florida's longest river; expansive salt water marshes; the Intracoastal Waterway; miles of beach; and thousands of acres of forest and woodlands.

Perhaps some of its small-town charm is responsible for the area's lingering — but unwarranted — reputation as a backwater, smokestack town. However, the metropolitan region was just shy of one million people in 1993 and likely will pass that magical mark before too long. High-end estimates by researchers at the University of Florida put the area's population at as many as 1.9 million people by 2020.

Part of the dramatic diversity of the city is probably due to its immense size — 840 square miles, the largest city, landwise, in the United States. A landmark consolidation of the city and county took place about 25 years ago. Neighborhoods are spread out, and vary from riverfront mansions dating back to the early 1900s to pricey, ultra-modern beachfront homes, to simple bungalows or sturdy middle-class brick houses.

With its ports, extensive rail lines and highways, Jacksonville is the center of a strong distribution network that links the South to the entire nation and international markets. And in the past few years, the area has garnered a reputation as an information services headquarters, with national companies bringing their backshop customer service and data processing operations here. The region has a longstanding tradition of banking and insurance concerns and now has become well-known for its health care facilities which include a satellite of the Mayo Clinic and the Nemours Children's Clinic which draws top pediatric specialists from the best hospitals around the country.

The Jacksonville Chamber of Commerce is targeting seven industries where the region already has a strong cluster of businesses and likely could develop areas of specialty even more: Healthcare Technologies, Information Services, Distribution, Transportation and Equipment, Instrumentation for Industry and Domestic Appliances, Building Products and Consumer Products.

A plan to revitalize the city's downtown is working its way through the political system. Dubbed "River City Renaissance," the plan calls for a $219-million bond issue to provide capital to upgrade the city's underlying infrastructure and redevelop existing areas for the arts, recreation and city government.

A LOOK BACK ❋

U p and down the St. Johns River, from downtown to Mayport near the ocean, broad shell middens — thick heaps of shells and bones — dot the landscape of its banks. Most people pass them and don't associate them with Indians. But the seemingly random piles of shells were deliberately laid by the area's earliest settlers as they discarded oyster shells and deer bones after foraging in the marsh and wooded areas. The middens are virtually Indian trash piles, and as archeologists sift through them they hope to learn how people in the Indian villages lived from day to day.

Some of the shell middens run for a quarter of a mile or more, allowing people to walk for hundreds of yards along the debris of the early Indian populations. These coastal shell formations are considered among the largest such deposits on the continent. A few burial structures — or Indian mounds — also remain. Many have been destroyed, some partially impacted and others remain intact. Among the latter is Shield's Mound, just north of Fort Caroline Road near Mill Cove. Reported to date back to A.D. 1300, what is called the St. Johns IIB Period, it may have been used to bury perhaps 150 people.

In 1988 and 1990, Bob Johnson of Florida Archeological Services Inc. conducted archeological surveys of the St. Johns Bluff area along the south bank of the St. Johns River. Johnson discovered in excess of 50 sites including Indian villages, burial mounds and campsites. Based on this work, the St. Johns Bluff appears to be one of the most populated areas in terms of prehistoric

deposits. What made the area attractive to the Indian population was its good dry land to live on, access to the river, the marsh systems and the forest, Johnson says.

Then in 1991, archeologists from the University of Florida surveyed the eastern coastal marshes of Northeast Florida. What they found would radically alter the conventional wisdom that had dictated the beliefs regarding the area's Indian settlements for decades.

Prior to the study of the Timucuan Ecological and Historic Preserve, researchers generally believed that year-round settlement of the area did not occur until about 2300 B.C. when evidence of Indian ceramics first appears. Early Indians, it was believed, migrated up and down the St. Johns River, stopping in the area for periods, and moving to the interior during other parts of the year.

But researchers led by Michael Russo discovered shell middens along the wetland borders of Fort George Island and Atlantic Beach that pushed coastal occupation as far back as 5700 years ago or 3700 B.C. Spencer's Midden, a shell deposit on the border of Atlantic Beach, is said to be the oldest coastal shell formation in east Florida and Georgia. The study, commissioned by the Timucuan Preserve, describes the early settlers in the coastal marshes as having survived on oysters, coquina and small estuarine fish such as herring, pinfish, croaker and catfish. They also subsisted on deer, lived in small villages, and likely used canoes to travel and communicate with other groups. More than 200 archeological sites were unearthed in the 46,000-acre preserve. Some are washed over in the ebb and flow of the ocean, revealed only at low tides.

Previously, historians relied heavily on the potential for agriculture among the Indians here.

That would have made them more akin to groups in other places in the Southeast where Indian societies were based on corn, beans, squash and the like. But the evidence just isn't there. More likely, Johnson says, with all the marine and estuarine resources, the early Indians didn't need to develop intensive farming, but relied instead on the river and marshes to live.

"Most of us believe now that the Indians were living here year round for several thousand years," said Johnson, who is a board member of the Jacksonville Historical Society. But much of the story of those earliest settlers still remains untold. Johnson says funds are needed to do more extensive research in order to craft a more detailed picture of the area's prehistory.

Visible remains suggest that significant habitation of the Jacksonville area really didn't begin until 3000 B.C. to 1000 B.C. when dramatic climate changes made the environment more hospitable. About that time the sea-level rose to its current height and the moist environment became drier. The lagoon system was essentially born. Oysters began to flourish in the area and the people who would subsist on them migrated here. The Indian population began to expand. By 1000 B.C., after evidence of ceramics appears, people were living in the area in great number. By 500 B.C. to A.D. 800 pottery designs and the materials used suggest not only that people were living here, but that tribes were passing through, trading as they went.

When Europeans arrived they named the Indians "Timucuan," based on the language they heard the natives speak. The tribal name used by the Indians themselves is unknown. They clustered in villages of circular thatched-roof houses. Each village was led by a chief, and groups of vil-

Archeological Dig at CPI

lages had a great chief over the hierarchy. Burial mounds were larger than those of previous cultures. Thirty-some villages are said to have been located at the mouth of the St. Johns River and along the coast.

The appearance of French sailing ships in the 1560s along the coast mark the beginning of the end of the Indian cultures in the region. Archeologists are able to trace the movement of the Indians as they fled the often hostile and disease-carrying invaders.

Visible signs of that transitional period of contact between the Indians and Europeans continue to be unearthed. In 1991, builders digging a retention pond for Holy Spirit Catholic Church on Fort Caroline Road in Jacksonville discovered an Indian burial site containing about two dozen

skeletal remains. The bodies, of old and young, were buried haphazardly — arms and legs twisted in all directions, and what made it more startling, some lying face down. Unlike traditional mounds, this site (dating to the late 1500s or early 1600s) was flat. Johnson said evidence suggests that the Indians died from an epidemic disease for which they had no immunity. As young and old alike began to die, the others, confused and frightened, buried them quickly, then fled.

After the site was surveyed and an Indian blessing was led by Native Americans, the retention pond was moved and the modern church completed. Historical researchers believe that 9 out of 10 Indians died within the first 100 years of the arrival of the Europeans.

Jacksonville's longtime Congressman Charlie

Bennett (who retired recently after 44 years of service) deserves a large share of the credit for the significant archeological studies that have helped reconstruct Jacksonville's earliest history. Bennett co-authored the National Historic Preservation Act of 1966 that made it necessary for all federally-funded, federally-licensed and federally-permitted projects to undergo archeological examination. Up to one percent of the budgets on such construction projects are to be set aside for historical preservation — one of the most significant pieces of legislation to affect archeology in the last 50 years. Bennett was also instrumental in passing a federal bill to protect unmarked human burials on federal and private land.

Also, it was through Bennett's efforts that the Timucuan Preserve was established by Congress in 1988 and put under the protection of the National Park Service because of its environmental and historical significance.

Residents and visitors who wish to learn more about the area's history may want to visit the Jacksonville Historical Center on the southern bank of the St. Johns River in downtown Jacksonville. Each wall of the center takes visitors through an abbreviated history of the area from pre-ceramic Indians to Jacksonville's first European settlers up through the establishment of the present-day city. Videotapes highlighting parts of the city's history are also available.

The historical society exhibit offers this brief history of the first European contact:

The European invasion of Northeast Florida began with Jean Ribault, who sailed from the Normandy coast in 1562 amid civil religious wars in France. Ribault landed at the mouth of the St. Johns River (then called River of May) on May 2, 1562. On exploratory missions, Ribault sailed up the coast as far as South Carolina, where he left a small garrison at present-day Parris Island.

On June 25, 1564, Rene de Goulaine de Laudonniere arrived with three ships carrying about 300 people, mainly Huguenots. The Timucuan chief welcomed them. The Timucuans and Frenchmen initially aligned. The Timucuans would help the French build a village and fort in a river bluff, and in return the French would offer military assistance to fight neighboring Indian groups.

The French named their settlement "la Caroline," or land of Charles, to honor the French king.

Spain had claimed much of Florida — some 200 settlements in area — and the Spaniards didn't take the French encroachment lightly. Spanish soldiers in 1565 made a surprise attack on the French fort, and much of the French force was killed.

During the two-century rule by Spaniards over the peninsula, they set up a network of Jesuit missionaries; however, their attempt to convert the Timucuans was futile.

The British descended on the region in 1764 when British East Florida's first governor, Colonel James Grant, arrived in St. Augustine and began recruiting settlers to clear the forest and establish slave farms. Grant started the construction of 'King's Road' to ease travel between Savannah, Georgia, and St. Augustine, Florida. A public ferry was necessary to cross the St. Johns River where it cut through the road. Kings Road still exists in Jacksonville and portions probably follow the original route.

While still under precarious Spanish control, Northeast Florida of the early 1800s was populated by Americans or British subjects. Major General Andrew Jackson came into the area to subdue raiding Seminole Indians and eliminate the British. In 1819, Spain ceded Florida to the United States.

By 1821, a small community, Cowford, had developed on the northern bank of the ferry crossing. That settlement, where in 1822 the largest landowners laid 20 blocks of streets, is the site of the city's current downtown. The fledging town was named after its first territorial governor, Andrew Jackson. Duval County, created in 1822, was named for the first civilian territorial governor, William Pope DuVal, descendent of the French Huguenots.

While the people of the area voted against statehood, nonetheless the majority of the territory voted in favor. Florida became a state in 1845 but joined the Confederacy in 1861.

During the Civil War, Federal troops occupied Jacksonville four times during the war, forcing many with Southern allegiance to evacuate. Homes and churches were used for respite for wounded Union soldiers, and federal gunboats patrolled the St. Johns River. Fort Clinch was surrendered to the North.

A myriad of Civil War artifacts have been discovered with the recovery of the *Maple Leaf*, a Union ship destroyed by a mine and sunk in the St. Johns River during the war.

The only major Civil War battle fought in Florida was the Battle of Olustee, 40 miles west of the city, where the Confederates were victorious. Elaborate yearly reenactments of the battle are staged at the site. An archeological survey of the area to definitively identify sites of the military camps and to unravel the story of the battle — and possibly the poor treatment of its black soldiers — is expected to be conducted soon.

A few vestiges of the Confederate past remain. At the foot of the Dames Point Bridge, is Yellow Bluff State Park, with a marker memorializing Confederate dead. Yellow Bluff Fort is on the National Register of Historic Places. In Confederate Park, just north of downtown, a marker was created for women who died in the war. Confederate General Joseph Finegan is buried at the Old City Cemetery, where each April the United Daughters of the Confederacy visit the grave sites and place Confederate and U.S. flags into the soil.

At the Old City Cemetery, in the northeast corner, are plots that were set apart for the use of Negro citizens. Black families who lived in Jacksonville since its founding are buried there. The Old City Cemetery, which lies at the center of Washington, Union, Ionia and Jesse streets and offers a rich look at the city's past is Duval County's largest repository of pre-1880s grave sites, according to *Jacksonville's Architectural Heritage: Landmarks for the Future*, an oft-referred to reference on Jacksonville buildings and neighborhoods. Hand-carved markers, cracked tombstones and wrought-iron fences give the old

graveyard a historic and ominous presence.

After the Reconstruction Era, the black community began to piece together a life of freedom. Blacks — many freed slaves who migrated here — outnumbered whites until 1910. And immediately following the war they found themselves in a period where they could exercise full rights of franchise. Blacks were able to succeed in business and politics.

Small groups of black professionals served as lawyers, doctors, businessmen, clergymen and skilled construction workers. In the late 1800s, Jacksonville lawyer Joseph Lee was the first black

municipal court judge here and served three terms in the Florida House and one term in the Florida Senate. Jacksonville blacks served as delegates to the state constitutional convention in 1868, and served as aldermen, city marshall, local tax assessor, police sergeants and other positions of authority, according to author and historian Barbara Hunter Walch, who has done extensive studies of Jacksonville's ethnic history.

Following the Civil War in 1868, a group of freed slaves paid $850 for a parcel of land at the corner of Broad and Ashley streets and built a school for black students, Stanton Normal

Jetties at the Mouth of the St. Johns River

School. One of the later principals of the school was James Weldon Johnson, born in Jacksonville in 1871 and later a black activist and well-known poet of the Harlem Renaissance in the 1920s.

In 1866, the African Methodist Episcopal Church founded Brown Theological Institute in Live Oak to help educate former slaves who had just recently been given the right to an education. The school was moved to Jacksonville in 1883 and renamed Edward Waters College. Edward Waters College is the oldest independent institution of higher education in Florida and is part of a Black Heritage Trail which marks significant historical sites throughout the state.

In the 1870s, Jacksonville's popularity as a resort destination for Northerners had come into full swing. A number of grand hotels provided accommodations. But besides its reputation as a vacation spot, other areas of commerce were

expanding. Among them was the port which has continued as an important part of the economy.

In 1879, Congress provided funds for the construction of jetties at the mouth of the St. Johns River at the Atlantic Ocean to promote trade through the waterways. Then twice in the late 1800s and early 1900s the river was dredged to allow larger ships to pass through. That opened trade with Europe.

On May 3, 1901, sparks ignited moss fibers at the Cleveland Fibre Factory on the corner of West Beaver and Davis street. What followed was mass devastation — Jacksonville's 'great fire' destroyed 2,300 buildings across more than 400 acres.

While you could hardly call such a tragedy a blessing, it ushered in a new era for the city. The rebuilding was swift and impressive.

Among those who came to rebuild the city was Northern architect Henry John Klutho,

Florida East Coast Railroad

whose legacy remains in the form of many prominent buildings and homes that adopted Frank Lloyd Wright's prairie style. Among Klutho's well-known structures is the St. James Building, built in 1910 for the Cohen Brothers department store. (Today, the mayor hopes to renovate the St. James Building and move City Hall to the center of Hemming Plaza, to help revive a once-thriving commercial area.)

An expanding railroad system and port helped rejuvenate the city and create a stronger commercial center. "The impact of port and railroad development stimulated the growth of wholesaling and to a lesser extent manufacturing for the region, both characteristics of the New South city," according to *Jacksonville After the Fire 1901-1919* by University of North Florida Professor James Crooks. "Jacksonville served as a regional distribution center for consumer goods.

One observer claimed the wholesale grocery houses alone exceeded in number those of Charleston, Savannah, and New Orleans, prompting the Board of Trade (now the Chamber of Commerce) to boost Jacksonville as the 'Gateway to Florida.'"

The city's banking and insurance concerns grew. The first life insurance company established in Florida was founded in Jacksonville. A black-owned company later known as Afro-American Life Insurance Co., was founded in 1901 and prospered until the 1970s. Later, in 1920, the founders of the Afro-American Co. established a black beach on Amelia Island, American Beach, that remains one of the last black beaches in the state. It also is on Florida's Black Heritage Trail.

By the end of World War I, Jacksonville had established itself as a strong Southern city.

According to *Jacksonville After the Fire:* Its population more than tripled from 28,249 in 1900 to 91,558 in 1920, property values increased almost eight times. The number of workers engaged in manufacturing rose four times; the value of their products, thirteen times. Bank deposits multiplied fifteen times, and bank clearings, reflecting local and regional commerce, increased almost fiftyfold. Exports were sixty-one times greater than a generation earlier; imports, 188 times.

Because of the natural resources available for the industry, shipbuilding and ship repair prospered. Other areas of commerce continued to flourish, and the federal government picked the area for several important military bases.

Naval Air Station Cecil Field, now scheduled for closure as part of military downsizing across the country, was established in 1942 on 2,600 acres of forested land. Mayport Naval Air Station was built in 1942 where the Atlantic Ocean meets the St. Johns River. In 1950, an aircraft carrier pier was constructed. In 1940, the Navy was looking for a major site for aviation training in the Southeast and thus was born Naval Air Station at Jacksonville on the city's Westside.

Jacksonville Ship Yards

Delores Kesler

Being a native of Jacksonville probably gives me a little different perspective than someone who has moved into the city. Growing up here, I accepted it with all its positives — the quality of life, the weather and the hospitality of the city. But I also made a clear-cut choice to stay here several times in my career when I was offered opportunities to move.

I grew up in rural Jacksonville in an area called Dinsmore, a dairy farming community just north of Jacksonville. I graduated from Paxon High School here and attended Jacksonville University.

In making career choices, I worked for several large corporations and at one time was offered the chance to move to Atlanta. I went to Atlanta and looked around. I opted to stay in Jacksonville. And that was the point where I said, "If I'm going to go into business myself, this is probably a receptive community for me to do it in."

The business I'm currently involved in, AccuStaff Incorporated, is a staffing service on the cutting edge of where businesses are focusing: How to manage their human resources.

We started a business here 14 years ago that has since developed into a national headquarters for our company. We have 51 offices in 15 states with the goal to grow into the other 35 states. When we started the business, the Jacksonville community was maturing and growing. This was a period when a lot of outside companies came into Jacksonville, locally based companies were growing and the University of North Florida was developing. Those were natural complements to the start up of a business.

Jacksonville served as a good springboard when we started spreading into the other communities in Florida and working our way north. The fact that Jacksonville was a Southeastern banking center and insurance headquarters...these were good business connections for us. From the aspect of an entrepreneur, I don't think I could have done a search and come up with a more welcoming and nurturing city than Jacksonville.

Delores Kesler grew up in Jacksonville and is president and CEO of a national staffing corporation, AccuStaff Incorporated.

After WWII, population increases led to growth in other industries such as food processing and manufacturing. Between 1940 and 1960, Duval County's population more than doubled, much of that growth in the undeveloped areas just outside the city limits. In those 20 years, the population just outside the city grew from 37,078 to 254,381.

Tourism in the area had pretty much faded and was supplanted by the development of tourism in south and central Florida. By the 1950s and 60s, the military had more or less stabilized. Banking and insurance companies began to flock here in greater number because of favorable state tax laws. Prudential Insurance Co. set up its 10-state regional office in Jacksonville in

1953. In 1954, its 20-story office building on the south bank of the St. Johns River was the tallest building in Florida. With 19 insurance companies, the city garnered the nickname "Hartford of the South." A symbol of the banking community, Florida's branch of the Federal Reserve System was in Jacksonville.

Industrially, there were several paper mills in the area, which are still operating. Shipbuilding waned, though some repair operations contin-

Xavier Del Juan Cain

I was born on Jacksonville's Westside in 1974 in a neighborhood known as Sweetwater. Historically, it was an important black neighborhood. What I find interesting is that all the street names are Biblical. They were named by the residents who lived there a long time ago.

Since then I've lived all around the Westside. But for me Sweetwater is home because that's where I started.

In the sixth grade I was in a gifted program and I was chosen to attend Stanton College Prep, a Jacksonville magnet school that prepares students for the best colleges in the country. In ninth grade I became interested in architecture. During a trip downtown to see Fourth of July fireworks launched from the Independent Life building (once the tallest building in Jacksonville), I remember looking up and realizing how tall it was. That played an important part in my decision to go into architecture.

Maybe I can do something creative and artistic and still create something that will serve people. Now I'm a sophmore at Carnegie Mellon University studying architecture. One of my goals is to become licensed in Florida. This is my home. I'd like to work for a firm that does renovations in addition to designing new buildings. I'd like to restore some of the structures here.

Then there's the idea of coming up with the next tallest building. For me, the thing about Jacksonville that is so unique is that the city is constantly changing. I want to be a part of that — help it go places it has never been before.

Xavier Del Juan Cain grew up in Jacksonville and is studying architecture at Carnegie Mellon University in Pittsburgh.

◄ The Prudential Building

ued; however, to date, repair docks located in downtown Jacksonville have disappeared and ship repair operations continue to shrink. Distribution operations through railroads, highways and the port continued to grow in prominence. For example, CSX Transportation traces its history in Jacksonville back to 1960 with the opening of the Atlantic Coastline office on 500 Water St. Through a series of mergers and expansions, CSX continued to grow into one of the largest employers in the area.

The 1960s were a critical period for the area politically. The community was disgraced by the disaccreditation of its public high schools in 1964, and bad government with a poor property tax policy were blamed for the school's failure. A slew of city officials were indicted by a grand jury on charges of bribery, larceny and perjury. Business leaders concluded that the corrupt government was stifling their bottomline. Underlying all of this was a massive flight of the population to suburban areas outside the city core, leaving the city on the brink of bankruptcy. Public outcry called for a massive reorganization of the city and county governments. On August 7, 1967, voters decided to merge Duval County and the city of Jacksonville in what became a landmark consolidation. As a result, Jacksonville became the largest city, landwise, in the United States. Many say the consolidation helped move Jacksonville foward.

In the 1970s and 1980s, a number of new large companies migrated to Jacksonville such as Vistakon, a subsidiary of Johnson & Johnson; American Transtech, a division of AT&T; and American Express. At the same time local companies and companies with regional offices here expanded.

◄ U.S. Gypsum Company

The Mayo Clinic

Jacksonville, while retaining its reputation as an insurance and banking and distribution center, now has emerged as a telemarketing and customer and financial services center and a regional hub for health care.

Like many cities, development has spread from a downtown core to suburban office parks and communities. A concentration of impressive, modern business towers and operations has developed on the city's Southside in areas known as Southpoint, along Interstate 95 and J. Turner Butler Boulevard, and farther south in Mandarin. But some businesses remain firmly committed to the downtown skyline, which during business hours remains bustling.

In the beginning of 1992, the four-county metropolitan area was on the verge of breaking the one million population mark with 940,891. Slow but steady growth will likely push the city over that mark before too long.

NORTHEAST FLORIDA'S NATURAL SETTING

O ne of the most compelling features of Northeast Florida is its natural setting. A series of distinct and beautiful landscapes exists within its boundaries: The ocean, beaches and dunes along its eastern edge. Coastal strand with ancient dunes. Vast stretches of saltwater marshes. The winding Intracoastal Waterway. The mighty St. Johns River and its myriad of creeks and tributaries. And in the west, thick forested areas, cypress swamps and farm pastures.

The ecosystems are so thoroughly integrated into the landscape that these natural settings are a common part of business and residential neighborhoods. You don't have to drive far to get away to nature — chances are you live there or it's in close reach. Many homes are built along the river, ocean or creeks and tributaries. And outdoor activities play a strong role in setting the pace of day-to-day life. Golfing, sailing, fishing, canoeing, hiking, scuba diving, surfing or just walk-

San Jose Country Club

The Acosta Bridge on the St. Johns River

ing and sunning on the beach are common activities.

But besides being a great source of recreation, the natural setting has many pristine and sensitive characteristics — some of which are being protected for future generations.

One of the strongest natural features of the area is the St. Johns River. The longest river in Florida that flows completely within its boundaries, it starts in the Kissimmee Prairie, west of Malabar, and flows northward for a distance of about 318 miles to its point of discharge into the Atlantic Ocean about 21 miles northeast of downtown Jacksonville. The St. Johns River is one of the few rivers in the country that flows north. Of Florida's major rivers, only the St. Johns and St. Marys rivers deposit into the Atlantic Ocean. The other rivers flow into the Gulf Coast. The St. Marys River is on the Florida-Georgia border on the northeast edge of the area.

The St. Johns, meandering with its thick loads of silt, is further unique among Florida's rivers in that its flora and fauna are a mixture of freshwater and marine organisms. Marine fishes enter the water at high-tides when salty waters are flushed in and there is little discharge of fresh water.

Jetties were built where an arm of the Atlantic Ocean reaches in with its tides to meet the St. Johns River. The estuary serves as a gateway for commercial cargo ships entering and exiting Jacksonville's international port and a gateway for Navy ships that are harbored just off the coast.

The river is home to endangered West Indian manatees, slow and gentle sea cows that can be seen surfacing with their large weighty bodies. Boating restrictions and low speed zones have been created to help prevent injury and death from collisions with boat propellers.

An extensive creek and tributary system exists around the St. Johns River. People like to explore the headwaters of the creeks in canoes. Black

Creek is a little bigger than most, but on narrow winding waterways like Durbin, Julington, Trout and Six Mile creeks, a canoer can get away from larger boats and quietly paddle for hours — sometimes without seeing a single boat. Instead, a vigilant canoer may spot alligators, river otters, snakes, turtles and ospreys.

Along the northeast coast of Florida are tremendously beautiful and isolated beaches all well within striking distance of about any place in Jacksonville. Several beach-lined state and city parks are located along the coast. One is Talbot Island State Park with its four miles of undeveloped pristine beach. North of the Talbot Islands is Fort Clinch State Park, where a massive fort — first built as a buffer against foreign invasion but later occupied by the Confederates and then the Union during the Civil War — sits along 8,400 feet of shoreline. Along 1.5 miles of beach at the north end of Atlantic Beach is Kathryn Abby Hanna Park, a city park with plenty of ocean access along high sand dunes. Inland, there are nearly 650 acres for hiking and camping or fresh-water fishing in lakes. Farther south is Guana River State Park which has a different type of beach. Instead of the hard-packed sand you find on many of the other

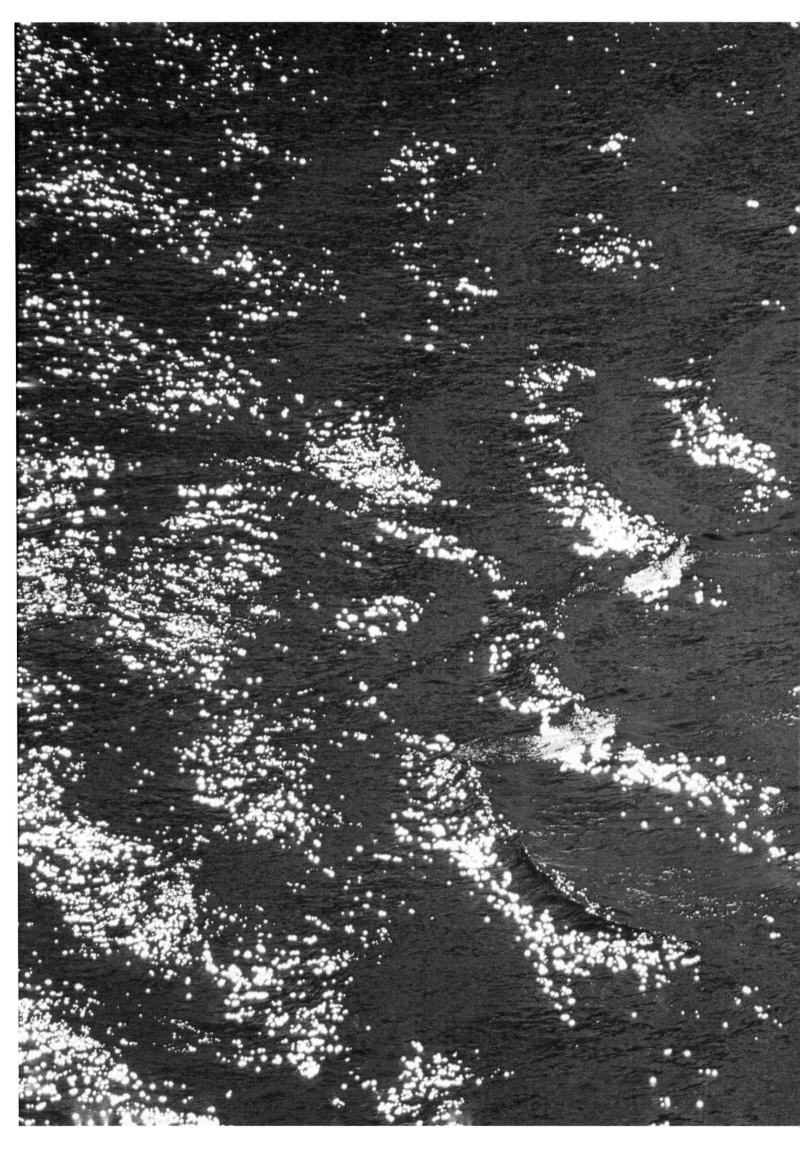

beaches, the southern Northeast Florida beaches are a thick hash of crushed coquina shells that your feet sink into as you walk along. Guana River Park, in St. Johns County, boasts some of the tallest dunes to be found in Florida — 35 to 40 feet in some spots, according to state park service biologist Bert Charest.

Dolphins feeding and playing in the ocean just off shore are a common sight. And the Northeast Florida ocean waters are the winter home of the endangered northern right whale, which migrates south from New England to this area in the winter months to breed. In fact, off-shore Jacksonville waters were included in a recent national designation of "critical habitats" for the right whales.

Off-shore fishing and scuba diving are popular because of a myriad of artificial reefs in the area. Everything from old football stadium press-box seats, barges, and pieces from local bridges have been carefully and systematically sunk deep in the waters to create new colorful reef habitats for fish — and scuba divers and fishermen.

In the beaches along the ocean, sea turtles come and nest. Loggerheads are the most common type, but there are also the endangered leatherbacks. An Atlantic Beach business owner organizes daily dawn patrols of the beach in residential areas so that the nesting sea turtle eggs can be protected and hatchlings can be guided safely into the ocean.

Just in off the beach, at the northern and

southern, less developed areas of the region, the first natural community you run into is coastal strand, a mixture of grassland and scrubby vegetation that has grown up along ancient sand dunes that stretch west. Within the coastal strand are vines of greenbrier or cat brier, redbay and sawpalmetto. By the time you get to the west side of highway A1A, the scrub gets thicker with several species of oak, palmetto and Southern Magnolia, a stunted magnolia that remains short and bushy. Along the coastal strand, the vegetation is wind sheared by whipping salt spray coming off the ocean. Under the thick, even overcoat of brush are undulating ancient sand dunes.

As soon as you get away from the strong maritime influences, the topography flattens and thick hammocks are dominated by several hardwoods including Virginia live oaks, Laurel oaks, hickories and some tall, stately magnolias.

According to Charest, a number of threatened and endangered plants and animals — such as the gopher tortoise and indigo snakes — live in this dry, harsh environment.

West of the hammocks are the marshes and then the Intracoastal Waterway, which runs from Miami to Maine, and winds through the Jacksonville area. On both sides of the Intracoastal Waterway is an extensive network of thousands of acres of saltwater marshes with their lush swaying spartina that are an important feature in the natural character of the area. The salt marshes run along the Intracoastal and on the ocean side around the St. Johns River and along its tributaries. "These are probably the most important communities that we have here in terms of uniqueness and productivity," Charest says. "They provide grand vistas and are extremely important natural nurseries for many

Little Talbot Beach

species for commercial and sport fishery." Many of the fish in the open sea spend at least part of their lifecycle in the salt marshes and tidal creeks that run through them. Saltwater marshes are considered among the most productive ecosystems. Salt-tolerant plants like saltwort and glasswort grow in the high marshes. Trees such as Southern Red Cedars grow along the marshes' edge. The uplands end abruptly at the salt marshes, and at areas like Little Talbot Island, it's a common sight to find the bows of Virginia live oak stretching out over the marsh.

The twice-a-day flushings by the highest tides in Florida are critical to maintaining this habitat and keeping out pollution. Canoeing and fishing in the marshes and tidal creeks are popular, and in the surrounding trees and grass the long-legged wading birds, such as the endangered wood storks, osprey, egrets and brown pelicans, are found. Oyster beds are found in the tidal creeks that run through the marshes.

A vast stretch of the saltwater marshes in the Jacksonville area were designated a federal pre-

serve in 1988 with the help of former U.S. Congressman Charles Bennett, who represented Jacksonville in Washington for 44 years. A sweeping 46,000 acres in the northeast section of the area were designated the Timucuan Ecological and Historic Preserve by the U.S. Department of the Interior. About 30,000 acres are wetlands. In addition to the breathtaking landscapes, historic forts and other cultural sites are within the preserve.

Offering quite a contrast to the marine influences, the western part of Northeast Florida

Charles E. Bennett

I t is thrilling to live in a bustling, business-oriented city like Jacksonville and find there excellent recreational, cultural, religious and higher-educational opportunities to fulfill every interest and need.

When I came to Jacksonville from Tampa in 1930 with my mother and father (while I was attending the University of Florida), I was struck with the uniqueness of my new hometown, as it was richly enhanced by the majestic St. Johns River. That river rolls its wide expanse of water even in the midst of the center city and eastward to the city's golden beaches on the Atlantic Ocean and interwinds through thousands of acres of marshland and wildlife habitat. And all of this is unbelievably close to fine residential development and significant harbor and industrial sites.

Jacksonville has important history. Here at St. Johns Bluff the 1564-1565 French Huguenot settlers, La Caroline, began the permanent settlement by Europeans of what is now the United States. It was the first movement to this land with religion as a purpose. Here was first recorded the birth of a child of European ancestry in what is now the United States. Jacksonville can accurately claim to be the only city in the United States which came both from the Renaissance and the Reformation. International battles were fought here between the French and the Spanish; and between the British and the American Patriots. In fact, it is the site of the Thomas Creek Battlefield (1777), the most southernly battlefield in the Revolution.

There are exquisite public golf links here, two national park facilities (Fort Caroline and the Timucuan Preserve) and several important museums and art galleries. Of the latter, Cummer Gallery owns and displays art 2000 years before Christ and about 2000 A.D., including works by Renoir, Whistler, Gilbert Stuart and other well-known painters.

So Jacksonville is a diverse and beautiful city, and I am very grateful to have spent most of my life among its down-to-earth, warm-hearted, wonderful population.

Charles Bennett represented Jacksonville in Congress for 44 years before retiring in 1992. Mr. Bennett is a professor of Government at Jacksonville University.

is characterized by forest, rural pastures and swamp lands. Much of the land is owned by paper companies and private owners growing timber to fuel the paper and pulp industries in the area. Just outside the city much of the land is still rural with horse farms, pastures for grazing and forest. In low areas, sandy soils create a flatwood ecosystem with longleaf, slash and loblolly pines. And the area is full of cypress swamps in lower depressed areas where the water tends to collect. There, cypress, bays, red maples and magnolias can be found. White-tailed deer, wild turkey and wild hogs are found in both ecosystems foraging and hiding.

A FAVORABLE BUSINESS CLIMATE

Jacksonville has always enjoyed natural attributes that create a strong business climate. In a strategic geographic position on the northeast coast of Florida, it serves as a gateway to the peninsula and a hub for the southeastern United States. Through its port, it is an arm to international markets. Waterways, in fact, have offered a critical economic advantage. The St. Johns River, the longest river within Florida's borders, runs through the city and meanders north to discharge into the Atlantic Ocean. A 38-foot deepwater port shuttles products such as paper, cars and groceries to international markets while huge cargo ships are seen cruising in along the jetties bringing coffee, bananas, automobiles and other items into the United States. In 1992, the Jacksonville port moved a record five million tons of marine cargo.

The Jacksonville Port Authority is adding a third marine terminal at Dames Point near its other facilities on Jacksonville's Northside Blount

Talleyrand

Cargo Ship Passes the Dames Point Bridge

Blount Island

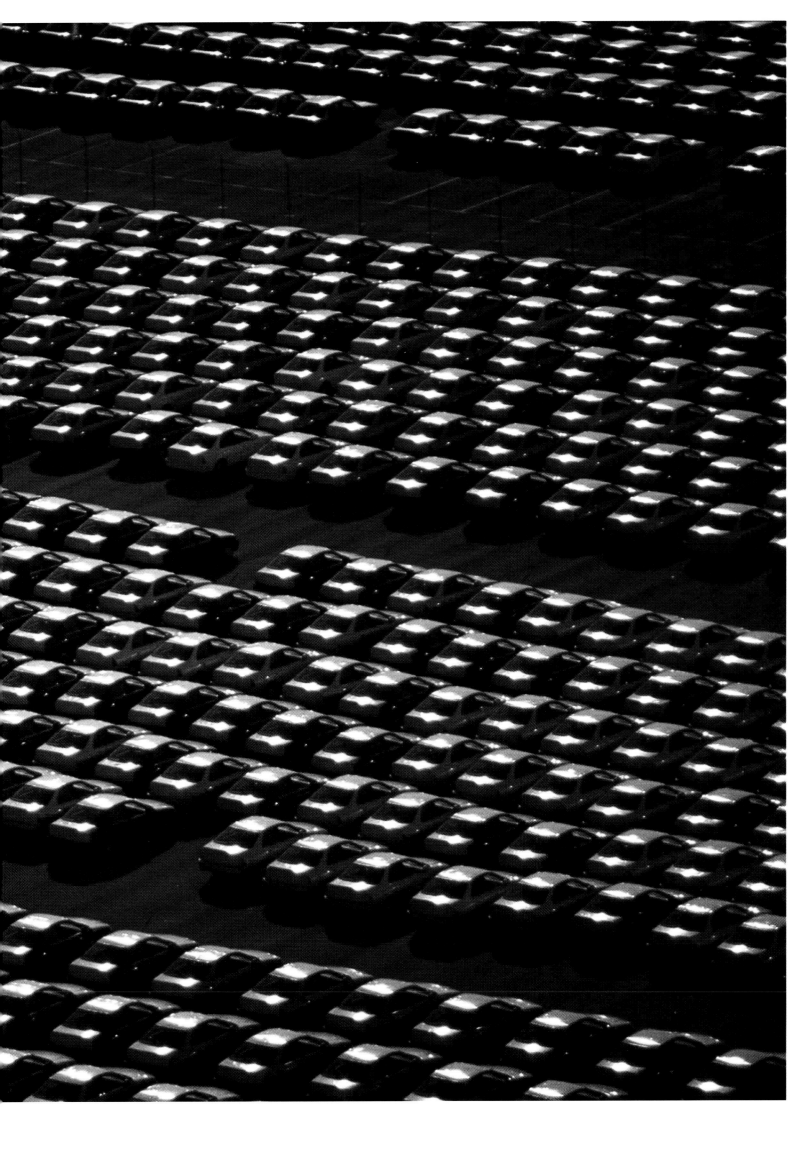

I-95 North

Island Marine Terminal. Land around its Talleyrand Docks & Terminals likely will be developed for truck terminals, warehousing, packaging plants and other related light industries.

An extensive land bridge from Northeast Florida to destinations throughout the continent exists along its three railroads — CSX, Florida East Coast and Norfolk Southern — and on major highways that originate in or bisect the city. Interstate 95, a major north-south highway artery of the eastern United States intersects the city. Interstate 10's eastern edge starts here and heads west, and Interstate 75 runs through the area just 50 miles west of downtown. All three transportation networks — water, rail and highway — are sometimes used in combination, moving products from Europe into the United States through the port and then loading it onto trains

for a three-day journey to California. The Jacksonville International Airport also serves to move products in and out of the region.

Besides the strong infrastructure for the distribution of products, Jacksonville has developed a reputation as one of the country's leading sites for industries that rely on electronic transfer of information: telemarketing, financial services and backshop data operations. AT&T's American Transtech, one of the largest telemarketing companies in the country is based in Jacksonville as is AT&T's Universal Card Services Corp. American Express and Merrill Lynch & Co. have located offices here and continue to expand.

The city long has had a tradition of being a center for banking and insurance. It has developed a regionally and nationally recognized cluster of health care facilities, including a Mayo Clinic

The Mayo Clinic

satellite and the Nemours Children's Clinic. The Jacksonville Chamber of Commerce's plan for economic development in the region identifies seven areas of enterprise in which the region has a strong cluster of existing businesses and the basis for further development: Healthcare Technologies, Information Services, Distribution, Transportation and Equipment, Instrumentation for Domestic and Industrial Applications, Building Products, and Consumer Products.

Add to this entire economic mix an emerging strong market. The metropolitan area was just shy of one million people in 1993. And with its small, but steady growth, University of Florida researchers speculate the area population — which includes Duval and its contiguous Clay, Nassau and St. Johns counties — may rise to 1.3 million by 2020 with high-end estimate at 1.9 million. In the last decade, the city grew at a rate of about 2.5 percent. While that's not a

large increase, it has been consistent. Unlike other Florida tourist areas where seasonal changes can be drastic, Jacksonville's population is fairly stable.

Cresting the one million mark is important for Jacksonville in terms of creating demand for goods and services. Local economist Louis Woods of the University of North Florida says

one million is a critical threshold. "It's sufficient to create demand to support lots of industries," Woods says.

And it's a young population with a median age of 32 years — under Florida's overall median 34 years. The local workforce is considered

generally well-suited for the service jobs that are increasingly becoming the predominate employment here. State figures in mid-1993 show that of the area's 422,900 jobs, 365,500 were service-oriented. Like other cities, Jacksonville is struggling to keep the number of higher-paying manufacturing jobs from shrinking.

As the Jacksonville economy moves into the

21st Century, efforts to continue to develop its clusters of enterprise excellence will continue. An Economic Development Council made up of government and business leaders was created during the summer of 1993 to help coordinate future growth. Soon, it will be expanded to include the adjacent counties to devise growth strategies for the region.

Meanwhile a grand scheme to revitalize much of Jacksonville's downtown core and outlying amenities is working its way through the political system. In 1993, the administration of Mayor Ed Austin developed a master plan called "River City Renaissance." It envisions a huge bond finance program to capitalize the renovations which would include renovating the Civic Auditorium for cultural events; improving the Gator Bowl football stadium (the site of an annual New Year's Eve Gator Bowl and the University of Florida and Georgia matchup); creating a new downtown library; enhancing the zoo and a myriad of other projects.

The plan to rejuvenate the city is the result of 20 months of study and review. In May of 1993, the Jacksonville City Council approved the River City Renaissance plan with some modifications. The mayor's office expects that many of the downtown revitalization projects will be underway by the end of 1993 or the beginning of 1994. The objective: Create a first-tier city.

The military — with three Navy bases in Jacksonville and a nearby base in St. Marys, Ga. — plays an important role in the economy with $1.25 billion in total annual payroll and 46,600 jobs. With the ongoing military closures and realignment, any city with military operations will have to brace for changes in the coming years.

Jacksonville is slated to lose Cecil Field Naval Air Station with its 9,274 military and civilian positions in 1999. And in the last three years, Mayport Naval Station has lost half its 34 ships. But with the closure of other bases around the United States, the local military operations will stand to gain from consolidations. The Naval Aviation Depot, an aircraft maintenance, repair and overhaul facility at Naval Air Station Jacksonville that employs more than 2,800, escaped closure on the latest round of military cuts, and, in fact, is expected to gain personnel in the consolidation of other depots. The sixth of 10 Ohio-class submarines slated for Kings Bay arrived in July 1993.

The Base Conversion and Redevelopment Commission, made up of business and political leaders, was put together in mid-July, 1993, to help transform the 23,000-acre Cecil Field from military operations to private business development. The base has four runways — one that has served as an emergency landing site for the space shuttle program — hangars and plenty of housing and office spaces that could be transferred to commercial use.

Former Navy personnel offer special

Homecoming at Mayport Naval Station

mechanical and aviation skills and it is hoped that a market for those types of skills will continue to grow. The economic impact of the military has always been significant for the area. The downsizing of the military will no doubt change the profile of the military community, but likely it will continue to be strong. Jacksonville Community Council Inc., a non-profit think tank that produces regular reports on issues facing the city, recently drafted recommendations to help the city through the military transitions.

Naval Air Station Jacksonville on 3,400 acres on the city's Westside, had about 15,282 employees in 1993, with 44 percent representing

civilian workers, according to the JCCI study. Among the key operations on the base are P-3C Orion aircraft patrol and training, helicopter squadrons and the Naval Aviation Depot (NADEP), which provides aircraft maintenance, repair and overhaul. P-3 operations are expanding. Moffett Field NAS's P-3 operations have been folded into NAS Jax as Moffett continues to disassemble since it was picked for closure in 1991. Other marine patrol and surveillance units are likely to consolidate at NAS Jacksonville. NADEP escaped closure in the latest round of military downsizing, and the depot will also gain personnel in consolidations. But NADEP, like other military repair operations, increasingly competes with private contractors for military maintenance work.

Naval Station Mayport, located at the mouth of the St. Johns River at the Atlantic Ocean had 14,099 employees in 1993, according to the JCCI study. The base can handle 40 ships and currently has one aircraft carrier, seven guided missile cruisers, seven frigates, two destroyers, one destroyer repair ship and one mine sweeper. Mayport was designed to handle conventional carriers, which over the years are being replaced by nuclear-powered carriers. Leaders are pushing for $280-million renovations to fit the base for nuclear carriers.

Naval Air Station Cecil Field, has 9,274 employees, but its 17 jet squadrons and much of its 8,500 personnel will be moving to three East Coast bases by 1999. Plans are underway to find the best alternatives for the 24,000 acres that include housing, runways and hangers. Many regions have rebounded from military closures by replacing military bases with airports, manufacturing operations, colleges or a number of other uses. The regional task force exploring the alternatives expects to draw up proposals before too long.

Just north of Jacksonville is the expanding Kings Bay Submarine Base near St. Marys, Ga., with Ohio-class Trident submarines and plans to up the number of submarines to 10. While Kings Bay is in Southeast Georgia, there's plenty of spillover in Northeast Florida. Many personnel and contractors who work on the base live or are headquartered in Jacksonville. And as the largest nearby city, Jacksonville attractions draw Navy personnel and their families.

William DeVaughn Sweet, Sr.

I was born in the small country town of Bartow, Florida, on July 16, 1909, a town I am proud to be from. The public schools in Polk County stopped at the eighth grade so I attended Edward Waters College in Jacksonville for ninth grade and completed the tenth thru twelfth grades at Florida Agricultural and Mechanical College in Tallahassee. I continued my education at Florida A&M and received my B.S. and M.A. degrees.

In June of 1930, I was contacted to teach printing at Stanton School in Jacksonville. (Freed slaves bought a parcel of land and started Jacksonville's first school for black children, Stanton, in 1868.) I joined St. Paul African Methodist Episcopal Church. There I was appointed Assistant Scoutmaster. Jacksonville was very supportive of scouting. Scouting grew very fast. I was named the first Field Scout Executive for the Suwannee District that included 11 counties. We grew to be the largest scouting organization in the South.

During that time, I was active with our teachers organization (the Duval County Teachers Association). In 1934, I was elected president. We cared for our association members who could not make it from one paycheck to another. Most teachers made $50 a month. Blacks — with a few exceptions — could not get loans from banks. On a Sunday afternoon, the executive committee met to discuss plans to help our members. I suggested that we form a bank, or ask a bank about possible low-interest loans for our teachers association. After long discussion, Dr. J. I. E. Scott came up with the idea to establish a federal credit union.

In 1937, the credit union became a reality. Just before summer break we had 33 members at $5 per share, which came to $165. Dr. Scott and I gave an additional $100 each and another $200 was donated. For a name, I decided to use the first two letters of each word in the name of our organization (Duval County Teachers): DUCOTE.

The organization that was started with $565 has more than $6.5 million today.

I've seen many things happen in Jacksonville. I've seen the barge carrying cows, horses and buggies, wagons and people across the St. Johns River. The Acosta Bridge was the only way to get to the Southside until the 1940s, and Durkee Ball Park was the only park in the city. I saw The Landing built at the foot of Ocean Street and many other things.

William DeVaughn Sweet Sr. started Jacksonville's first credit union for black teachers. He is a long-time trustee of Edward Waters College and former chairman of the board of the Clara White Mission.

While the Naval Aviation Depot is among the largest manufacturers overall, Jacksonville's largest private manufacturing company in terms of employees is Vistakon with its 1,500 workers. A small niche in medical-related manufacturing is emerging here with such companies as Vistakon, a Johnson & Johnson contact lens maker; and Xomed-Treace, a Bristol Myers Squibb company that makes surgical equipment.

The largest non-manufacturing operation, according to the Jacksonville Chamber of Commerce, is AT&T, with its Universal Card Services and American Transtech subsidiaries here employing 8,000.

Northeast Florida certainly makes its mark in Florida's overall economy. Twelve of Florida's largest public companies in terms of revenue are headquartered in Jacksonville and 16 of the state's largest revenue producing private companies are here, according to *Florida Trend* magazine's 1993 guide to Florida companies.

Florida's largest public company in terms

of revenues is Winn-Dixie Stores Inc., the country's fourth-largest grocery chain with more than $10 billion in annual sales. Winn-Dixie, which has been headquartered in Jacksonville since 1939, has continued to increase its earnings despite heated competi-

tion from other grocery store chains and the growing number of price clubs like Sam's Club and Pace Warehouses. Florida's largest bank, Barnett Banks Inc., also is headquartered here. Barnett continues to strengthen its position as the state's top bank, buying out other Florida banking operations. In 1993, Barnett held 28 percent of all deposits in the state, and that figure is expected to grow. The second largest bank in the state, First Union National Bank of Florida, is also headquartered in Jacksonville.

Eleven Jacksonville companies that were among Florida's top public companies in terms of revenues in 1993 include: American Heritage Life Investment (insurance), Family Steak Houses of Florida Inc. (restaurants), Florida East Coast Industries Inc. (rail transportation and industrial parks), Florida Rock Industries Inc. (concrete, gypsum and plaster), FRP Properties Inc. (trucking), Independent Insurance Group Inc. (insurance), Koger Equity Inc. (real estate investment), Koger Properties (office park developer), Riverside Group Inc. (insurance holding company), St. Joe Paper Co. (timber, paper mills) and Stein Mart Inc. (department stores).

Sixteen of the state's top 100 private companies in terms of revenues in 1993 headquartered in Jacksonville are: Lil' Champ Food Stores Inc. (convenience stores), National Merchandise/Pic N' Save (wholesale and retail merchandiser), Gate Petroleum Co. (retail petroleum products, building materials and real estate), RPC Inc. (heavy equipment, truck sales and service), Cain & Bultman Inc. (wholesale distributors), Mac Papers Inc. (fine paper distributors, envelope converting), Coggin-O'Steen Investment Corp. (auto dealerships, real estate and hotels), Beaver Street Fisheries Inc. (food distribution, import and export), The Haskell Co. (architecture, engineering), Scott-McRae Group Inc. (auto dealerships), King Provision Corp. (supplier to Burger King restaurants), Southeast Atlantic Corp. (soft drink bottling and distribution), W.W. Gay Mechanical Contractor (mechanical contracting), SUDCO Inc. (household products, moving and storage), Vogue and Body Shops Inc. (retail clothing) and Physician Sales & Service (medical supplies distributor).

Jacksonville's business climate continues to draw new companies. The region has been a favorite with corporate relocations because of its large pool of workers, its relative low wages and its relatively low cost of living. Jacksonville's average home price of $115,633 is below other big cities in Florida.

Just look at the companies that have moved here in the last few years. In 1990, AT&T chose Jacksonville for its new product, AT&T Universal Card Services Corp. Starting with 1,500 employees, they added another 500 in 1991. One year later, the new concern won the prestigious Malcolm Baldridge National Quality Award. Two years before AT&T Universal Card opened shop in Jacksonville, American Express brought a 1,500-person operation to town, and

the Association of Tennis Professionals picked the pristine coastal area just west and south of Jacksonville in St. Johns County for its international headquarters.

The list of newcomers continues to grow. And established companies are expanding. Merrill Lynch, the nation's biggest brokerage, has moved three operation centers here that process mutual funds, mortgage products, life insurance and annuity products. The company is adding its third building to a Southside campus. CSX Transportation has increased its presence. Vistakon added a third facility in 1993, and Computer Power Inc., which handles mortgage records, is in the midst of expanding its facility along the St. Johns River just southwest of downtown.

Medical and health care delivery facilities have begun to cluster in the region. A big boost, so far as national recognition for the area, came in 1986 when the highly-regarded Mayo Clinic chose Jacksonville for its first extension outside Rochester, Minn. (The only other Mayo satellite is in Scottsdale, Ariz.) The late J.E. Davis, one of the city's patriarchs and co-founder of grocery-giant Winn-Dixie, donated land for the clinic in an expansive wooded area near the Intracoastal Waterway. Now, the Mayo satellite has doubled in size to 310,000 square feet with 138 staff physicians. The Mayo Clinic chose Jacksonville in part because of its ideal location — a link to the Southeast and to foreign countries east and south of the United States. The satellite clinic recently announced its plan to eventually redouble the size of its Jacksonville operations.

In the fall of 1990, another prestigious medical institution, Nemours Children's Clinic,

The Mayo Clinic

opened its new 11-story facility along the south bank of the St. Johns River and brought in some of the finest pediatric specialists from around the country. Besides those facilities, Jacksonville has four large medical centers: Baptist Medical Center, Memorial Medical Center, St. Vincent's Medical Center and University Medical Center, the latter which serves as a teaching hospital for the University of Florida. Baptist and University work closely with Nemours on children's health. Other health-care-related manufacturers are gravitating here.

The workforce in Jacksonville has always been one of its advantages. Historically, it has been perceived to be a low-labor-cost commu-

nity that generally, like the rest of Florida, has a non-union, right-to-work philosophy. But business leaders say other intangible qualities draw companies to the area's workforce, among them, a strong work ethic. "I think that has to do with Jacksonville as a magnet, pulling a lot from rural Georgia and rural Northeastern Florida," says Delores Kesler, president of AccuStaff Incorporated, a national personnel service. "That work ethic is somehow associated with rural markets."

Kesler says Jacksonville can no longer be characterized as a low-skill or low-cost labor market as businesses continue to develop training here. Large companies here spend a great deal of money for

in-house training and programs set up by Florida Community College at Jacksonville. Partnerships abound between business and the educational community to improve the workforce. Among the most vivid demonstrations of such partnerships is FCCJ's newly opened Donald D. Zell Urban Resource Center, which offers a variety of job skills training, upgrading and assessment. Many large and small companies have used FCCJ's Urban Resource Center as a place to custom design training for positions.

Like other cities, Jacksonville realizes that there can be gaps in matching employees with the needs of area businesses. Communities survive and develop during tough economic times

by having the skills that match the newly developing employment bases. Local business and education leaders are working hard to establish training and other vehicles to keep the workforce current.

Area companies realize that it's never too early to devote attention to the future workforce. A number of Jacksonville companies have formed partnerships with Duval County public high schools, middle schools and even grade schools. For example, Blue Cross & Blue Shield of Florida Inc. established a satellite claims office at Andrew Jackson High School, where students are gainfully employed by the company. Barnett Banks set up a minibank at Matthew

Gilbert Middle School, where students make deposits and withdrawals in quasi-real accounts. KPMG Peat Marwick has a finance program and helped start a recycling business at the school that is run by a 12-year-old CEO. It turns a tidy profit that is funneled back into a Saturday reading program.

Another example of addressing future workforce issues is the Private Industry Council of Jacksonville's summer program for low-income youth. Teenagers from poor neighborhoods spend part of each day during the summer in school classes and at a job that helps gives them a head start in the world of work.

The business and education community is starting to tackle what is perhaps the most seemingly intractable workforce problem: The unemployed and so-called unemployable. Dubbed the "third tier," programs to bring these people back into the work place are likely to be in place in the next few years. "It's the enigma to everyone: How do you get your arms around it? How do you spend your money wisely?" Kesler questions. "How do we bring them up, give them the tools to be able to move into that low-skilled category and then provide opportunities to advance?"

Although Northeast Florida does have a number of pricey resorts in Nassau and St. Johns counties, it lacks the concentration of tourism that typifies South Florida and the Orlando area. However, the workforce in the area is more stable than in the seasonal, tourist centers of the state. And the slow, steady growth of population seems to be balancing well with the growth of companies here.

Gregg Troy

I've lived in Jacksonville 16 years. I'd only been to Jacksonville one time previously when I swam as a competitor in the Florida Junior Olympics in 1965. I came here in 1977 to take a position as swimming coach at The Bolles School. The area has always had a good swimming tradition with a lot of outstanding athletes. When I came, I came with the intention of continuing that, knowing that Jacksonville had been a leader in competitive swimming in the South.

For my profession, there are a wealth of athletes in the area, and Bolles provides a great educational institution for those athletes to excel athletically as well as giving them the background they need to go further in their lives professionally. Because of the uniqueness of the situation at Bolles — having a boarding program — we've been fortunate to have athletes from around the world come here to train.

That's even more appealing with the upcoming Olympics in Atlanta. Because of the proximity to Atlanta, Jacksonville provides a great training atmosphere for people who want to compete.

I think it is a unique area that provides a lot of the opportunities of a large city, but at the same time retains a lot of the good qualities of a small southern town. We live on the Southside right down the street from school and enjoy the convenience to the beach and a climate that is favorable to being outdoors most of the year. When I have time, I like to fish and play golf...both of which are excellent in the area.

Gregg Troy is the swimming coach at The Bolles School, a private college prep school. He has coached 15 Olympic swimmers, including four Bolles graduates who won medals in individual events at the 1992 Olympic Games in Barcelona, where Troy coached Thailand's team.

RECREATION AND CULTURE ✺

acksonville's warm climate, its mild winters and year-long sunshine, make it an ideal setting for outdoor sports and recreation. The international headquarters for the PGA TOUR and the Association of Tennis Professionals both are located in Northeast Florida.

Early each spring, more than a hundred of the world's best golfers and thousands of their fans converge at the Beaches area for the Players Championship at the Tournament Players Club in Ponte Vedra Beach. The Players marks the last stop on the PGA tour's Florida leg. Resorts along the coast fill for the week-long golf event that first moved to Sawgrass in 1977. The Players Championship is considered the fifth most important tournament of the year, trailing the U.S. Open, the British Open, the PGA Championship and The Masters.

The PGA Tour headquarters moved to Ponte Vedra Beach in 1979. Now, an international Golf Hall of Fame — the World Golf Village — is under construction off Interstate 95 in St. Johns County and expected to open in 1995. The World Golf Village will include the International Golf Museum, the LPGA Golf Hall of Fame, the PGA of America World Golf Hall of Fame, an IMAX theater, the national headquarters of PGA Tour Productions, a PGA Tour golf academy, a golf course, a national sports medicine facility and a 500-room resort and conference center. The World Golf Hall of Fame in Pinehurst, N.C., is being moved to the Northeast Florida golf complex.

San Jose Country Club

You don't have to be a professional to enjoy the golf. Northeast Florida has been called golf's best-kept secret with 45 public, private, semi-private and resort courses. And many of those courses have been designed by the who's who of golf architecture. Donald Ross, designer of Hyde Park on Jacksonville's Westside, also designed the oldest links in Florida, the 1916-crafted Ponce De Leon course in St. Augustine. Pete Dye designed Amelia Links on Amelia Island Plantation, and Ponte Vedra's own Mark McCumber designed Golf Club of Amelia Island and the course at Queens Harbour Yacht & Country Club in Jacksonville. Queen's Harbour is one of a myriad of pricey area residential communities built around golf courses.

With so many courses, players have the opportunity for variety. Most courses don't get crowded like the fairways at other big golf destinations where the pace is slow and congested. The warm climate, with an average annual temperature of 71, means the courses can be kept in great shape.

The Association of Tennis Professionals moved its international headquarters to Ponte Vedra Beach in 1989 and since expanded its facility. The general manager of the ATP predicts that its grounds will continue to grow as does its reputation among professionals as a top-notch facility for training and rehabilitation from injuries. In the fall of 1992, the facility began hosting the ATP Senior Tennis Tour Championship, which features top former players such as Bjorn Borg, Rod Laver and Stan Smith. Tournament managers say they expect to continue to host the annual Seniors championship. Besides that, the ATP regularly plays host to the up-and-coming professional tour players in Challenge Cup events.

Northeast Florida is also host to the Bausch & Lomb Championship in which some of the world's leading women players compete at the lush Amelia Island Plantation resort. Like the PGA tournament, the women's tennis competition becomes a week-long event that draws people from throughout the Southeast. Jacksonville area residents often rent beachfront condominiums for the week and mix great tennis viewing at the tree-shaded clay courts with long walks on the beach, gourmet meals and perhaps some amateur tennis matches of their own.

College football is followed with religious fervor in the South and the Jacksonville area is no exception. While Jacksonville has no college football teams of its own, the University of Florida Gators, the Florida State University Seminoles and the University of Georgia Bulldogs all command near-fanatical allegiance.

An annual Florida vs. Georgia matchup at the 80,377-seat Gator Bowl football stadium has deep roots in the city, which turns orange and blue and red and black for the fall game. The

The Gator Bowl

Jacksonville series between the two teams dates back to 1933 when a group of local businessmen convinced the schools to play alternating home games here instead of at the school's campuses in Gainesville and Athens. Situated on the northern edge of Florida, just south of the Georgia border, the Jacksonville game is a big draw and a guaranteed weekend party for fans from both teams. It is one of the few college football games where seats are split evenly between schools.

Boosters from each side hold gigantic pep rallies and parties throughout the weekend. Historically, college fraternities have run footballs from Athens and Gainesville to Jacksonville before the game.

Vince Dooley, former Georgia coach and current athletic director, decided to move the 1995 rivalry to Sanford Stadium in Athens, Ga. But after that, the game moves back to Jacksonville through the turn of the century.

Another local college football tradition is the New Year's Eve Gator Bowl. Organizers of the bowl vie for a top spot among the post-season matchups. With renovations of the stadium, organizers of the game hope to be in a good position to vie for even the national championship game. Currently, the bowl takes the third-place Southeastern Conference team and matches them up with a highly-ranked opponent.

The Gator Bowl tradition also has deep roots in the city, with the first post-season game played in 1946. Having brought the annual Florida-Georgia match up here more than a decade earlier, business leaders met

in the fall of 1945 and quickly put into motion plans to bring the college bowl game to town. Charles Hilty, owner of the Sun Crest Soft Drink Co., and Raymond McCarthy, owner of 7-Up Bottling Co., met and then formed a committee to bring a bowl game to the city to stimulate business and tourism. Two top committee members, Walter McRae Sr. and Charles Thebaut, were big Gator boosters and thus the name Gator Bowl was born. Wake Forest defeated South Carolina (26-14) in the inaugural Jan. 1, 1946, bowl game.

A drive for a National Football League expansion team has consumed the city for more than a decade. The effort reached a fever pitch this past summer as the NFL owners readied to announce two cities to be awarded expansion teams. Plans for massive renovations of the Gator Bowl were tied to the NFL drive. But during the eleventh hour, the group of business leaders trying to bring the pro team to town, Touchdown Jacksonville! Ltd., decided to pulled their bid after reaching on impasse on a Gator Bowl lease agreement with the city. City leaders later revived the effort to put Jacksonville back in the running for a team, but, at this writing, the outcome remained uncertain. Regardless, $49 million in stadium improvements are planned to help keep the college games here.

Jacksonville's Wolfson Park is home to the Double-A affiliate of the Seattle Mariners and has served as host to farm teams for a number of other major league organizations. The tradition of professional baseball in Jacksonville goes back to 1904 with the

The Greater Jacksonville Kingfish Tournament

SALLY league. Hank Aaron, baseball's all-time home run hitter, played in Jacksonville for the Jacksonville Braves when the SALLY league team played at Durkee Field at 8th Street and Myrtle Avenue (now J.P. Small Park).

In addition to baseball, minor league teams in other sports such as hockey and basketball have been established here.

Plenty of other sporting events are scheduled throughout the year. Started in 1977, the River Run 15,000-kilometer road race attracts world-class runners and has grown to as many as 6,500 finishers. The 9.3-mile course starts at the Gator Bowl and winds through neighborhoods along the river and includes a challenging incline and decline over the lengthy Hart Bridge. Popular 10-mile runs along the beach are held annually in the winter and summer, and a host of other runs are sponsored by the local track club and running shop.

For avid fishermen, the annual Greater Jacksonville Kingfish Tournament offers great sport and competition. Each July, fields of up to 1,000 boats — everything from 16-foot skiffs to 40-foot sport fishermen — head out from the Pablo Creek Marina in search of the prize catch. Each afternoon, throngs of spectators line viewing stands at the marina to watch the boats trail in and lift out fish for official weigh-ins. So far, the record catch is a 50.7-pound kingfish.

The waterways surrounding and bisecting the city are year-round havens for fishing — whether it's deep sea fishing over sunken reefs 50 miles offshore, or standing barefoot along the edge of the ocean with a surf rod as the tide slowly moves in bringing whiting, croker, black drum and an occasional kingfish.

Other water sports such as sailing, scuba diving, surfing and kayaking are popular. Divers enjoy the myriad of artificial reefs offshore and the intricate underwater caves and caverns in an

Mayport Fishing Boats

extensive natural spring system in small towns outside the city.

Jacksonville Beach has begun to establish itself as host to professional and semi-professional beach volleyball tournaments. The barefoot, two-to-four-player-team, dive-in-the-sand competitions are played at a beachside volleyball park completed in 1992. Large crowds gather at the beachside courts for the national competitions.

Greyhound races are held year round in the region during four-month seasons rotating among three kennel club operations in Jacksonville, Orange Park and St. Johns County. Satellite feeds and off-track betting are held at the idle clubs during the races. In 1992, the races grossed about $125 million, and payouts to bettors averaged about $2 million a week.

In addition to sports, music and art events are held throughout the year.

Metropolitan Park, along the river just east of downtown near the Gator Bowl, is the site of the annual Jacksonville Jazz Festival held the second weekend of each October. The internationally-renowned event has featured top jazz performers including Grover Washington, Miles Davis, Dizzy Gillespie and George Benson. About 130,000 jazz enthusiasts from all over the country throng to the four-day event which is produced and managed by local public radio and television station WJCT. A popular event that kicks off the jazz festival is the Great American Jazz Piano Competition held at the historic Florida Theatre where piano soloists compete for the top award. Blues Festivals have also been held in the park as well as at a beachfront amphitheater in Jacksonville Beach.

During the spring and summer, the Jacksonville Symphony Orchestra sets up in

Crawford A. Easterling

Naval aviation was well established at Naval Air Station Jacksonville in the years immediately preceding World War II, and the Naval Station at Mayport and Naval Air Station Cecil Field were built during the war.

Jacksonville enjoyed a superb reputation in the Navy when, as a young officer just out of flight training, I was ordered to my first squadron here in 1953. I was not disappointed. It was a delightful city in which to live and a strong bond with the Navy existed then as it does today. I married a Jacksonville native and the first of our two children was born here.

While assignments during the career that followed included duty stations in much of the United States and in Europe, comparisons were invariably made with Jacksonville. When orders came for another tour of duty here, they were received with much excitement as our family felt we were going "home."

Each time we returned, the city had grown and the number of bridges across the St. Johns River had increased. But the friendship and caring that had become hallmarks of the citizens of Jacksonville remained constant. Duty here culminated with command of a fighter squadron at NAS Cecil Field and command of an aircraft carrier at the Mayport Naval Station.

The fact that the Navy payroll is the largest in the city and that the payroll of Navy retirees exceeds that of active duty personnel is a testimonial to the continuing popularity of Jacksonville into retirement. As the end of my career approached, there was never any doubt as to where we would settle.

Jacksonville's growth during the years of my association has not been limited to that of area and population. The quality of life has been enhanced by the growth of cultural, educational, medical and recreational facilities. Both the city and the Navy have shared in that growth.

Crawford Easterling is a retired Vice Admiral in the United States Navy. He retired in 1986 while serving as the Commander of the Naval Air Force, U.S. Pacific Fleet.

The Starry Nights Series

Metropolitan Park for an outdoor series featuring top popular artists. The Starry Night Series has hosted Dionne Warwick, Judy Collins, Maureen McGovern, John Denver, Tony Bennett, Roberta Flack and Mary-Chapin Carpenter. Patrons bring blankets, folding chairs and picnic baskets to relax outdoors for an evening of music. Boat owners often just sail or motor up to the river bank along the park and enjoy the music while anchored in the water.

Now in its 44th season, the Jacksonville Symphony has performed with world-class performers such as Luciano Pavorotti, Itzhak Perlman, Jessye Norman, James Galway, Kathleen Battle and Pinchas Zuckerman. With the introduction of Roger Nierenberg as music director in 1984, the symphony has expanded in size and vision. The JSO employs 50 full-time musicians and many part-time players.

The St. Johns River City Band is the official state band of Florida and presents lively concerts of jazz, Broadway and popular brass music year round. Each year, Florida Community College at Jacksonville presents its FCCJ Artist Series, including music and dance at the Civic Auditorium and Florida Theatre. The riverfront Civic Auditorium, home of the symphony and site of other cultural events, is scheduled to undergo a $24 million renovation — an upgrade that is part of the recently developed River City Renaissance, a $219-million bond issue designed to create a major facelift for the downtown area.

Indeed, plans for revitalization are in the works for other of the city's arts and recreational facilities. A master plan to transform the Jacksonville Zoological Park into a world class facility by the turn of the century is underway. The first of a series of new exhibits — designed to create a sense of the animals' natural habitats and allow visitors close viewing — opened in the spring of 1992. Resembling a grazing area in southern Africa, Mahali Pa Simba, Swahili for "place of the lion," is a one-acre setting that houses three lions. The 73-acre zoological park on Jacksonville's Northside is home to two of Florida's endangered panthers who were taken from Big Cypress National Preserve. Only 50 to 60 Florida panthers are left in the wild. Among the zoo's other distinctions, it is responsible for the most black jaguars bred in captivity in a single zoo. The first breeding of a Toco Toucan in the western hemisphere took place there.

The zoo first opened in historic Springfield just north of downtown in 1914 with the humble "collection" of a single red deer fawn. As the zoo grew it moved to its present site in 1926. School children raised money for its first major animal purchase: An Asian elephant. Like other non-profit organizations the zoo constantly faces fundraising challenges. But influential citizens have continued to support the zoological park.

Jacksonville's fine sampling of museums and theaters includes the oldest art museum in the city, the Jacksonville Art Museum, opened in 1924. Throughout the years, an incredibly wide range of works have been displayed there, from the Great Pharaoh Ramses II exhibit to the watercolors of Andrew Wyeth and the photographs of Annie Leibovitz. The Wyeth exhibit in 1992 marked the only showing of his works from private collections in the Southeast, and included many pieces from his personal holdings. The museum's permanent collection includes paintings, drawings and sculptures by renowned artists such as Picasso, Nevelson, Anuszkiewicz, Calder and Raffael. Works by regional artists such as Louise Freshman Brown are also highlighted. The museum holds classes for children, lectures and other workshops to provide involvement in the arts for the entire community.

In 1958, Ninah May Holder Cummer, wife of Arthur Gerrish Cummer whose family had made their fortune in lumber and banking, created a foundation to enhance the cultural community in Jacksonville. The Cummer Gallery of Art and Gardens situated along the St. Johns River in Riverside has 11 galleries that cover artistic trends from 2000 B.C. to 2000 A.D. The gallery stands on the site of the former Cummer house with the original formal gardens along the river. An English garden was first laid out in 1910, and an Italian garden modeled after one in the Villa Gamberaia near Florence, Italy, was created in 1931. The

Jacksonville Art Museum

gallery hosts lectures, gallery talks, tours, concerts, holiday events and programs for children from throughout the region.

Jacksonville is one of five cities in the United States with a Karpeles Manuscript Library. David Karpeles, after making millions in the residential real estate boom in California in the 1970s, began pursuing his passion — collecting historic documents and original handwritten letters of great men and women of the past. He has set up five museums where the public can come view the documents without paying an admissions fee. The historic relics are rotated among his museums in Montecito and Santa Barbara, Calif., New York City, Tacoma, Wash., and Jacksonville, where Karpeles restored a Christian Science church just north of downtown for the museum. Among the documents that have been displayed: the original manuscript of Abraham Lincoln's Emancipation Proclamation; the Declaration of Allegiance of all Indian tribes to the United States; pages from Mozart's *Marriage of Figaro*; a 12th century vellum document signed by Pope Lucius III, empowering Knights Templar to protect pilgrims embarking on the Holy Crusades to the Middle East; the Constitution of the Confederate States of America and the proposal draft for the Bill of Rights.

On the south bank of the St. Johns River is the Museum of Science and History, expanded in 1988 to 74,500 square feet. The Museum houses the Alexander Brest Planetarium, the 16th largest planetarium in the United States. Public and school programs are presented under its 60-foot dome. Permanent collections at the museum include a historical exhibit featuring Civil War artifacts retrieved from the wreck of the steamboat *Maple Leaf*, which sank in the St. Johns River in 1864; an exhibit on the Timucuan Indians and

Joan S. Carver

In the past 30 years there has been a remarkable transformation in the city of Jacksonville — politically, demographically, economically. A sleepy, blue-collar, somewhat parochial, highly segregated southern town has become a bustling, pace-setting city with opportunities for both black and white citizens.

Jacksonville was in crisis in the 1960s. White citizens were fleeing to the suburbs, the tax base was eroding, race relations were tense, the infrastructure was decaying, the entire school system had been disaccredited and corruption was rampant. The archaic overlapping city and county governmental structures were neither effective nor responsive.

The depth of the problems helped bring change. There was a sense of excitement and a spirit of community as civic leaders, the media and many average citizens — labeling themselves "white hats" — battled the so-called "black hats," the forces of the status quo. The results were stunning: the establishment of a consolidated city/county government — one of the few in the nation — and the defeat of most incumbents. The overlapping governmental jurisdictions and the numerous authorities, boards, commissions and officials were replaced with one government headed by a mayor and a 19-person council. Along with the changed structure came leaders who brought to government energy, enthusiasm and a desire to move the city forward.

In the 25 years since a consolidated government was adopted, much progress has been made. Services have improved, the school system has been accredited, the downtown redeveloped, the cultural life of the city expanded and opportunities in the public and private sectors increased for minorities and women. Population has increased and the city has grown economically.

The challenge for the next 25 years for both leaders and citizens will be to maintain and improve the quality of life in the face of increased population pressures and economic competitiveness. The spirit of togetherness that brought a new consolidated form of government will be needed in coming years as we struggle to have the best of the small-town atmosphere and the big-city advantages.

Joan Carver is dean of the College of Arts and Sciences at Jacksonville University.

their ancestors who lived along the St. Johns River in the pre-Columbian era; and displays focusing on the first European explorers of the area.

On the campus of Jacksonville University in Arlington is the Alexander Brest Museum. It features an eclectic collection of art from the school's benefactors and is host to showings of students and many local artists.

The Florida Theatre downtown is often a showcase for live performances of musicians, dance, theater and comedy. It was built in 1927 as a movie palace and vaudeville theater and was restored, reopening as a performing arts center in 1983. Offering a fairly intimate setting, it seats 1,978. Theatre Jacksonville, which seats 311 in an art-deco style building in the heart of San Marco, is one of the oldest continuously producing community theaters in the United States. FCCJ is constructing a four-building fine arts center with a 550-seat auditorium and 180-seat theater and art gallery at its South Campus. It is expected to be completed by early 1996.

Sensing a void in the cultural community as far as African-American and other ethnic plays were concerned, Jacksonville native Ron Parker created The Rennaissance Theater of the Performing Arts in an Arlington strip mall at the site of a former movie theater. The new troupe has performed *Sizzle, Will the Real Mr. Jones Please Stand Up, The Colored Museum Fences* and *A Soldier's Story*.

The Arts Assembly of Jacksonville Inc. was created in 1972 to nurture and coordinate cultural efforts in the area. Among other programs, the Arts Assembly distributes grants to artists and art agencies and each year presents ARTS MANIA, a weekend arts festival for all ages that attracts more than 100,000 people. It's the only festival in the Southeast with emphasis on hands-on arts education and activities for physically and emotionally disabled children and adults, according to the Arts Assembly. The Arts Assembly publishes a comprehensive annual directory of arts agencies, galleries and the like in the Jacksonville area which is available by request.

William Slaughter

I live "at the beach," "across the street from the ocean," "on the edge of the continent." Different ways of saying the same thing. Just saying one of them, wherever else I find myself, makes me feel closer to home.

On the J. Turner Butler Bridge, Jeanie, my wife, spots an osprey taking off with a mullet, that it fished out of the Intracoastal Waterway, in its talons. "I wonder what the world looks like from the mullet's point of view," she says. "A minute ago it was in its element. Now it can't possibly know where it is."

Jacksonville must have looked like that to me when I arrived from Indiana in 1972 to teach at the then brand new University of North Florida. I couldn't possibly have known where I was. But I've long since forgotten what being out of my element must have felt like. My students past and present friends greet me everywhere I go. Some things don't happen unless you stay in one place long enough. Life is more than a passing through.

"I keep words./My wife keeps birds." The start of a poem I'll likely never finish, but which has given the fifty-year-old, two-story, gray-shingle house that Jeanie and I live in in South Jacksonville Beach its name. Or rather, its names: "The Bird House. The Word House." A man ought to live in a house his own age, I'm fond of saying. And I do. With Jeanie and her exotic birds.

Other cities I've lived in: New Orleans and Seattle; London; Alexandria, Egypt; and Beijing, China. All of them exotic, in different ways, like Jeanie's birds. When asked about my work, teaching and writing, wherever else I find myself, I hear myself say: "The reason I go away, as often as I do, and travel great distances, is so that I can come home, again, different somehow."

A poem of mine, "The Hostage," written when I was a much younger man than I am now, ends like this: "Place is important, after all." I still believe that. Jacksonville is.

William Slaughter is a poet and an English professor at the University of North Florida. He was a Senior Fulbright Lecturer in China and Egypt.

JACKSONVILLE'S MOSAIC OF NEIGHBORHOODS ✸

Jacksonville is a patchwork of neighborhoods — steeped in character and with deep historical roots — that are vastly distinct from each other. This diversity is partly the result of the city's large 840-square-mile land mass: Neighborhoods spread far apart can easily develop unique characteristics. Everything from historic Springfield with its early 1900s Queen Anne-style homes to Mandarin with its modern, quickly developed suburban cul-du-sacs can be found in the Jacksonville area real estate market.

Like nearly everything about this region, water plays a key role in neighborhoods. Individuals and families often choose to live near the water — whether it's a house built along the mighty St. Johns River or the meandering Intracoastal Waterway, or a home butting up to sand dunes on the Atlantic Ocean or built with a dock on the quiet, gentle creeks and tributaries that wind through the landscape. The variety of places to live can't help but satisfy nearly every taste: Older homes in secluded rural settings; turn-of-the-century homes listed on the National Register of Historic Places; bungalows or riverfront mansions; new developments and patio homes; condominiums and townhouses. More than 145 public parks are maintained in the city adding to its natural ambiance and providing sports fields.

A low cost of living often attracts newcomers to the area with an average home price of $115,633 for a 2,200-square-foot dwelling, according to 1992 figures from the Jacksonville Chamber of Commerce.

A brief look at a small sampling of the mosaic of neighborhoods shows the rich quality of life:

Springfield

Riverside

Riverside/Avondale. In 1974 a group of concerned neighbors formed Riverside Avondale Preservation, an ongoing concerted effort to maintain the historic qualities of the area such as elegant homes built before and after the great fire of 1901. The riverfront provides the setting for grand homes that define the 8-square-mile neighborhood that was the city's elite and exclusive community prior to WWII. With homes dating from 1900 to 1935, Riverside touts the largest collection of prairie-style homes designed by Henry Klutho. In 1985 it was Jacksonville's first nationally designated historic district. Avondale was built up in the 1920s. Old homes with driveways for horse and buggy still exist.

In the adjacent neighborhoods, housing ranges from elegant riverfront mansions to small one-story bungalow homes and historic apartment buildings. They continue to be popular neighborhoods in part because of their proximity to downtown — 10 minutes away. Major interstates are close, but there's still a friendly small-town ambiance. Sixteen parks and the river maintain a natural setting around the homes. A park in Riverside at the corner of Park and Post streets with duck ponds and huge old oaks and maples marked 100 years in 1993.

A revival of the oldest portion of Riverside, the northeast quadrant along Post and Myra streets, is underway. Unique homes with attractive plasterwork and elegant fireplaces are being restored. As with the historic Springfield neighborhood to the north, people with the talent and patience for renovation can purchase homes for a moderate price.

Within the residential setting are several small retail districts with specialty shops and

Bethel Baptist Church in Springfield

restaurants. A shopping area called Five Points at the corner of Park, Post and Lomax streets was built in the early 1920s and remains vital with antique shops, clothing stores, a well-known wine shop and private art gallery. Featured recently in *Southern Living,* the Shops of Avondale, in the heart of the neighborhood on St. Johns Avenue, has outstanding restaurants and clothing stores. Some of the most talented florists in the city have shops here. A third shopping area at Park and King streets, smaller than the other two, has original street lights. The shopping areas in Avondale and at Park and King streets recently underwent renovations and landscaping.

Springfield. In the early 1900s, Springfield was considered the premier neighborhood, and it thrived with the growth of the city after the devastating fire of 1901. Prominent citizens built

grand Queen Anne and Colonial Revival homes that lined the moss-fringed, oak-shaded streets just north of downtown. Among them is a 1901 Colonial Revival home built at 25 East First St. for the founder of Barnett Bank (now Florida's largest bank). Northern architect Henry Klutho saw a great personal opportunity in coming to Jacksonville to help rebuild the city after the fire. His own prairie-style residence was located at 30 W. Ninth St.

More than 100 blocks of the area (1,800 structures) were designated a National Historic District in 1987. More than two-thirds of the homes in Springfield were built before 1921, according to *Jacksonville's Architectural Heritage* by Wayne Wood, a primary reference on the history of Jacksonville's neighborhoods. Wood's book explains that the area draws its name from a natural spring in a field that was at the site of today's Fourth Street.

Like other urban neighborhoods, Springfield, alas, has undergone periods of decay and decline. Successful efforts to restore the beautiful homes contrast with the neighborhood's reputation as a rundown, high-crime area. The maligning of the area sometimes unfairly overshadows its charm and unique offerings. But despite the problems, tenacious revival continues. It has been a dream neighborhood for couples who want a low-cost home. Financial assistance is available, and many homes have sold at less than half the square foot price of comparable homes in other Jacksonville neighborhoods. Preservationists formed Springfield Preservation and Restoration in 1975 and continue to prod the neighborhood forward to reverse its decline. Periodic SPAR Tours of historic homes draw hundreds of people to the neighborhood.

San Marco

Another neighborhood in easy reach of downtown is **San Marco**. The neighborhood is best known for its triangular, quaint shopping district, San Marco Square, at the intersection of Atlantic and San Marco boulevards. It is named

John Dyrssen

For the last 34 years, I have resided in the Isle of Palms area, a waterfront community that allows me to keep my boat at a dock in the backyard. I can leave my dock and fish in the Intracoastal Waterway, the St. Johns River or the Atlantic Ocean. I have a charter fishing business and fill my days fishing with my many friends. We certainly have no shortage of fishing areas in Jacksonville.

My wife of 40 years, Gretchen, is an avid painter and a member of the Garden Club. We have three children: sons, Stephen and Paul; and daughter Marilea. It is a tribute to Jacksonville that all three continue to live and work here.

Yes, like every city it has its warts, and I quip about them as much as anyone; however, on the balance, it comes out on top of most of the cities I have visited or lived in.

I was born in Lexington, Missouri, a stone's throw from the Missouri River. I grew up loving the water and especially enjoyed fishing and duck hunting. After a stint in the Marines following high school, I worked for the Vendo Co. (closely aligned with Coca-Cola Bottlers) and traveled the United States — all 50 states and virtually all the major cities.

When I was offered the sales manager position, I was to move to Atlanta, home of the Coca-Cola Co. However, I was familiar with Jacksonville since I had visited it many times, both as a Marine when stationed at Parris Island and in business travels. I convinced my employers that I should reside here. After all, Jacksonville had good air service and was a travel hub. It was not incidental that I was familiar with the beautiful St. Johns River, the ocean, and all the other great fishing in the area.

I have never regretted my choice.

John Dyrssen is a retired executive with the Vendo Co. who has lived in Jacksonville Beach for 34 years and operates a charter fishing boat.

for the famous St. Mark's Square in Venice, according to *Jacksonville's Architectural Heritage*. The focal point is a tall fountain at its center. The area's trendy shopping and bistro-style outdoor restaurants also were featured in *Southern Living*. The charming district has an art deco theater, Theatre Jacksonville, a setting for live performances. Built in 1937 with funds from Carl Swisher of Swisher Cigars, in 1991 it was placed on the Register of Historic Places. Homes in the area are a mix of Spanish, Georgian and Colonial/Tudor. Many were built between the late 1920s and WWII. San Marco's art deco facades and proximity to downtown make it a popular neighborhood for professionals.

Just to the south of San Marco is **San Jose**, the neighbor identified by its central San Jose Boulevard, a wide, attractive thoroughfare through a neighborhood of the same name. Key to the identity of San Jose is Epping Forest, which got its start when a 1920s riverfront mansion once owned by the du Pont family was refurbished into a yacht club. The surrounding property was then converted into an upscale, stylish community. Mediterranean-style homes with clay tile roofs are abundant in the area as are sturdy, brick homes along quiet residential streets off San Jose Boulevard. The Bolles School, a college prep school that draws students from throughout the world, is located in San Jose.

South of San Jose is **Mandarin**, an area about 45 minutes from downtown that has boomed

with new apartment and single-family home developments. Historically, it was the site of a Spanish mission and later a British settlement. Harriet Beecher Stowe, author of *Uncle Tom's Cabin*, moved here in 1868 and set up a winter home on a 30-acre orange grove, according to Jacksonville's *Architectural Heritage*. Stowe's house was destroyed in 1916. For years, the area was a small citrus community. In some places, the flavor of rural Mandarin with its canopies of large oak trees remain. Many streets have become long commercial stretches, and an abundance of shopping is available at the nearby Avenues Mall, a huge modern complex. Orange Park Mall is not too far away across the Buckman Bridge on the other side of the St. Johns River.

J. Turner Butler Boulevard is generally a quick direct route from the southern part of Jacksonville to its beaches. The **Beaches** — Atlantic, Jacksonville and Neptune — have drawn families since the early 1900s when summer coastal homes began cropping up along the shore. Simple cypress-shingled beach houses were built around the train stations along a track used to transport commercial fish into town. Constructed in the late 1800s and early 1900s, homes were modeled after Cape Cod structures: Wood-shingled, simple designs with long verandas and breezeways to take advantage of the ocean air. They weren't fancy homes, just enough for a comfortable summer. For years it was a ritual for families to pack up at the end of the school year and

Jacksonville Beach

Fernandina Beach

move to the beaches for the duration of the hot summer. At the beginning of September, families would just pull the door shut and move back into town. More families poured out to the beaches with the completion of Atlantic and Beach boulevards — linking the beaches to Jacksonville — in 1910 and 1949 respectively.

Many of those Cape Cod homes still stand. But now modern homes lived in year-round have been built throughout the Beaches. Trendy blocks of shops and restaurants are set along the eastern stretch of Atlantic Boulevard, the dividing line between Neptune and Atlantic beaches. An impressive 450-acre oceanfront park, Hanna Park, lines the northern end of Atlantic Beach.

Atlantic, Neptune and Jacksonville beaches are all within Duval County, but each has an independent mayor, city commission and some public services. When Jacksonville and its outlying county suburbs consolidated in 1968, the Beaches had voted to remain independent. Among some Beaches residents there has been a ongoing movement — which has gained quite a bit of momentum of late — to split off and create a separate county: Ocean County. With all the politics involved, such a development may take quite a while.

To the north and south of the Jacksonville beaches are two beach resort communities: Ponte Vedra Beach in St. Johns County to the south and Amelia Island in Nassau County to the north. **Ponte Vedra** is popular with upper-income retirees and is the setting for second homes of many well-to-do from around the country. Multi-million-dollar homes line the ocean, and condominiums and golf course communities have been developed in the area. Locals take advantage of several resorts in the area: Ponte Vedra Inn and Club and the more modern Lodge & Bath Club and Marriott at Sawgrass. The international headquarters of the PGA Tour and the Association of Tennis Professionals are located in Ponte Vedra Beach. Among the slew of famous golf courses is the Tournament Players Club with its well-known Stadium course.

Amelia Island, just north of Jacksonville, is a combination of history, luxury, and industry. Set between the ocean and lush oak-lined salt-water marshes, the island is a resort getaway with Amelia Island Plantation and a Ritz Carlton. Condominium and housing developments with tennis and golf are a big draw. And each spring, top women tennis professionals compete there in the Bausch & Lomb Championship.

Historic Fort Clinch, built originally for protection against foreign invaders, but later occupied by the Union during the Civil War, is spread out against the coast. A quaint shopping district with great restaurants is at the center of Fernandina on the island.

On Jacksonville's eastside, inland from the beaches, is **Arlington**, a sprawling, diverse neighborhood. A range of incomes and residences are represented there: Everything from pricey custom homes along the river and country club developments to modest middle-and lower-income homes in its small neighborhoods within the neighborhood. There is truly a plethora of neighborhoods in Arlington with strong-knit identities. Just consider that there are about 40 community and civic associations there. Arlington's Regency Square, one of the city's largest shopping centers, draws people

Louise Freshman Brown

When I was young, the song, "There's a Place for Us," from *West Side Story*, had particular meaning for me. Florida was the place for me from the first time I was here in the 1950s. I also identified with artists like Georgia O'Keeffe for many reasons, but initially because her identification with New Mexico was immediate during her first visit. My fascination with time and place attracted me to Gauguin and his Tahiti and Matisse's connection to Morocco. My mother, also a painter, was drawn to Santa Barbara.

And my place is Jacksonville.

Over the past 30 years, I have been creating a body of work that explores widely disparate elements of natural and human-made environment. Twenty-two of those years have been in Jacksonville. I have completed numerous series, such as the figure, the landscape, marine life, native plant forms, architecture and still life. These compositional and expressive issues are both physically and emotionally related to my environment.

Jacksonville landscape is open space. Marshes and the river are everywhere, plant life is exotic, the sky seems larger and the colors more intense. I still get the same rush of excitement I had as a child driving from the North to Jacksonville.

In 1991, I had a solo exhibition at the Jacksonville Art Museum. The students I have taught and continue to teach and the artists whose ideas and dialogues I have shared were there. I saw the collectors who have acquired my work and my family who are my toughest critics. There were many of my colleagues from the University of North Florida where I am a professor of art and the teachers and students from Duval County schools where I spent four years as Artist in Education. There were also those who knew me only through my images.

In their midst, it was at once surprising and vividly clear that I really am a Jacksonville artist.

Louise Freshman Brown is a Jacksonville artist who is a professor in the Department of Communications and Visual Arts at the University of North Florida.

Dames Point Bridge

from throughout the city. Jacksonville University, a small private liberal arts college, is located along the river on the western edge of Arlington. University of North Florida's campus is set off St. Johns Bluff just south of the area. Historic sites and a federally protected natural preserve are also located on the western edge of the neighborhood, which is connected to downtown via an expressway that runs across the Mathews Bridge. Jones College, a small business school, is located at the foot of the bridge.

The Dames Point Bridge (an impressive and architecturally lauded span bridge formally known as the Napoleon Bonaparte Broward Bridge) connects Arlington to Jacksonville's **Northside**. The bridge's recent completion has spurred growth in the area outlined by highways such as Interstates 95 and 295. The Jacksonville Port Authority's Blount Island terminal, the Jacksonville International Airport and industrial park JAXPORT; and the Jacksonville

Zoological Park are all located on the Northside. The Northside is often considered a solid blue-collar neighborhood, but there's a mix of real estate including upper-income homes and developments. Much of the land on the Northside remains rural and undeveloped. Natural settings in the saltwater marshes are preserved for recreation on Little Talbot and Big Talbot islands and Huguenot Park. The latter is popular for driving onto the beach. Boaters enjoy the rivers and streams with public ramps and private docks. Small towns within the Northside such as Oceanway retain distinct identities.

The **Westside** is considered a stable, middle-income community of neighborhoods linked to small communities such as Baldwin, Marietta, Maxville and Whitehouse. Jacksonville's largest military complex, Jacksonville Naval Air Station, is located on the Westside as is Naval Air Station Cecil Field, which is scheduled to close in the latest round of military contractions. Long commercial strips exist along Cassat, Edgewood and Lane avenues and Roosevelt and Blanding boulevards. Roosevelt Mall, Cedar Hills and Paxon shopping centers offer convenient shopping. Strong neighborhood and athletic associations provide activities for youth and adults. The western portion of Duval County is characterized by forest, pastures and swamp lands. Wooded areas of pine and hardwoods offer a rural contrast to the city to the east.

Considered Jacksonville's old-money neighborhood, **Ortega** is located on the eastern edge of the Westside. Families migrated into Ortega from the once stylish Springfield when the latter began to decline. Grand homes line the river, and streets are shaded by large, lush trees. Ortega is home of the exclusive Florida Yacht Club and Timuquana Golf and Country Club, which recently have come under fire locally and nationally for their historic practice of excluding black members. Nearby newer neighborhoods are Venetia and Ortega Forest.

To the south of the Westside is **Orange Park** in Clay County, one of the fastest growing counties in Florida. New housing developments have sprouted up throughout Orange Park which still retains some of its rural charm. Blanding Boulevard continues as a long commercial strip in Clay County and Orange Park Mall draws shoppers from all over the area. Boating is popular along the St. Johns River and Doctors Lake. Much of the undeveloped parts of Clay County remain wooded and rural.

Robert E. Johnson

When I moved to Jacksonville in 1970 at the age of 23, I was immediately impressed by the immense size of the city, a city bisected by a broad gentle river, the St. Johns. Having grown up in a rural agricultural community in coastal Virginia, I was not immediately sure that I could learn to like big city life.

I had come to Florida with an interest in scuba diving and archeology. While serving in the U.S. Air Force in the Vietnam War, I read a book called *Invitation to Archaeology*, by James Deetz, a book I brought back from Southeast Asia. After studying archeology under Dr. Charles H. Fairbanks at the University of Florida, I returned to Jacksonville to start my own archeological consulting firm.

Some 15 years later, archeology is my profession and still my passion. In 1985, I developed a keen interest in the archeology of the Jacksonville area — precisely because of what little actually was known about the area. I received two grants from the state of Florida through the Florida Community College at Jacksonville to conduct archeological surveys along the St. Johns River from Reddie Point to Mayport. These investigations discovered over 50 sites ranging from small camps to extensive villages and even Indian burial mounds, proving that the area had been more extensively occupied during prehistoric times than was previously believed.

Following our surveys, the National Park Service conducted an extensive study of the Timucuan Ecological and Historical Preserve in which many more sites were identified, some in excess of 5,000 years old. The investigations by our team, the Park Service and others, is going to be instrumental in rewriting the prehistory of the Jacksonville area.

I am excited about this future not only as an archeologist but also as a citizen of Jacksonville. This city has a bright future and I am looking forward to being part of it.

Robert E. Johnson is founder and president of Florida Archeological Services Inc. and has conducted many private and public archeological investigations in Northeast Florida.

SCHOOLING

Education is at the heart of a city's well-being because of its critical role in shaping the future workforce and enhancing the character of its citizens. Like public school systems in many large urban areas, Duval County's public schools have had their struggles. But ongoing efforts to improve the quality of education and alleviate racial imbalances are showing results. Prominent among the strategies is a program of specialized magnet schools where students can focus on particular subject areas such as math, the sciences or foreign languages.

A significant boost to the public schools system is coming from local businesses. Clearly, Jacksonville business leaders are assuming an ever larger role in helping to create a quality public education system. "We definitely are making strides in the direction of saying, Okay, this isn't strictly a challenge for the

school system or the educational system. It's obviously something where businesses have to become partners,'" says Delores Kesler, a member of the Jacksonville Chamber of Commerce workforce committee and CEO of AccuStaff Incorporated, a staffing service.

Businesses are aligning themselves with the schools through a variety of creative and impressive programs. For example, Blue Cross & Blue Shield of Florida Inc., the state's largest health insurer, has created a first-of-a-kind program in Duval County by setting up a satellite claims office

on the second floor of Andrew Jackson High School, an inner-city school just north of downtown. Students-cum-employees work shifts processing medical claims for entry-level wages. Some of those students upon graduation are hired full-time by Blue Cross which pays for, but insists they go on to, college. Blue Cross also works with other school students at their Southside offices.

Barnett Banks Inc. set up a mini-bank operation at Matthew Gilbert Middle School, located in the heart of a low-income neighborhood. Students work as tellers and managers, and the entire student body can make deposits and withdrawals of pseudo-dollars doled out for good grades and good behavior. The soft money can then be used to purchase items from a catalogue company created at the school. Also at Matthew Gilbert, KPGM Peat Marwick has set up an accounting and business education program. Along with Covenant Industries, the Big Six accounting firm also helped students start a recycling company that has been turning tidy profits under the leadership of 12-year-old chief executive officers. A legal studies program has been set up by Jacksonville's black bar association.

Florida Community College at Jacksonville with a number of financial service companies are involved with high school students, offering college-level business courses and hands-on training through internships.

Partnerships with business of all types throughout the city helped launch a system of magnet programs in 1991 to draw students with

special talents or interest. Students can focus on math, engineering, foreign languages, African-American studies, sports, the arts and a number of other areas through the concentrated programs.

The magnet programs were a response to a 1990 federal court order, forcing the Duval County Schools to achieve greater racial integration. By drawing students across town from different neighborhoods, it is hoped the magnet program will create racial balance among the student body. But the magnet programs have also developed unique learning opportunities.

The Duval County school district is the 16th largest in the nation. In 1992, it had 116,000 students enrolled in 148 public schools. The system's 6,000 teachers are certified by the Florida Department of Education and administered by an appointed superintendent chosen by an elected seven-member school board. A number of impressive new schools have been built and others completely renovated in an ongoing $314 million construction program. A master plan for as many as nine new schools has been proposed to ease classroom crowding, but negotiations over the plans are being conducted with the local NAACP because of the racial equity concerns.

PRIVATE SCHOOLING

There are some 90 independent schools in the Jacksonville area, ranging from very small to large institutions — some affiliated with churches. Several of the private schools are well-regarded for their college preparatory programs. Here's a sampling:

The Bolles School, which accommodates students from kindergarten through the 12th grade, draws students from all over the world. The main campus in San Jose is a cluster of tree-shaded

Mediterrean-style buildings along the St. Johns River and middle school students attend the Bartram Campus in a pastoral setting. Originally a military and boys school, Bolles was founded in 1933 by Richard J. Bolles, a real estate mogul. It has a residence program as well as serving the local community. Episcopal High School, founded in 1966, is a Christian college preparatory school for students grades 6 through 12. It's located on 58 acres along the St. Johns River off Atlantic Boulevard. The school has about 600 students with an average class size of 20. St. Johns Country Day School in Orange Park in nearby Clay

County accepts students from pre-kindergarten through 12 grade. Set on 25 acres across from Doctors Lake, it is a non-denominational school named after the St. Johns River and founded in 1953. St. Johns Country Day School has an average enrollment of 600 students drawn from throughout Northeast Florida. Bishop Kenny High School, a Catholic school that serves grades 9-12, was founded in 1952 with the consolidation of three Catholic high schools in the area. Located about two miles east of downtown Jacksonville on the site of a former Spanish fortress, about 1,100 students a year are enrolled in the school.

HIGHER EDUCATION

There are a number of colleges and post high-school training programs in the Jacksonville area. University of North Florida traditionally has been one of the smaller universities among the nine schools that make up the State University System of Florida. But UNF is growing. When the university first opened its doors in 1972, it offered classes just for the upper two undergraduate levels and master's degrees. In 1984, it began admitting freshmen and sophomores. The student body has continued to grow, starting with 2,000 students in 1972 and rising to about 10,000 in fall 1993. Officials say it may even double by the end of the next decade. There are 329 faculty and 1,350 full-time and part-time staff. UNF offers 45 undergraduate degree programs and 24 at the master's level. It began offering its first doctoral program, the Ed.D., in 1990. Among the ways UNF has tied into the local business community, the College of Health has continued to expand to help meet the needs of the region's burgeoning health care industry. UNF's Small Business Development Center and Business Incubator Group provide assistance to small businesses in the area. The university's 1,000-acre campus is tucked into woodlands 12 miles southeast of downtown Jacksonville.

Florida Community College at Jacksonville is the second largest community college among Florida's 28 community colleges and is the 10th largest in the country. It started as Florida Junior College in 1966 with 2,610 students — a record for a beginning class. Today, FCCJ has four campuses and off-site classrooms throughout the city, serving 90,000 part-time and full-time students enrolled in its college credit courses, training and enrichment programs. After two years, graduates can move into Florida's nine full-time universities. FCCJ's Urban Resource Center provides employment training for all levels of positions from basic job skills to executive level programs. It's an important link among business, government and educational groups in the community.

Jacksonville University is an independent, private college on a 260-acre campus on the St. Johns River in Arlington. With an enrollment of about 2,500, J.U. includes colleges of arts and sciences, business and arts with bachelor's degrees in more than 50 areas. The school offers a popular Weekend Studies College to give working adults a chance to finish their undergraduate degrees. The Institution of World Capitalism was recently founded on the campus. Among other programs, it includes an undergraduate program in entrepreneurship, teaching students from the United States and abroad the basics of starting and running a company.

Edward Waters College, the only historically black institution of higher learning in the Jacksonville area, is a four-year private liberal arts school about two miles northwest of downtown. Edward Waters has an average enrollment of 650 students. The school was founded in 1866 by the African Methodist Episcopal Church as Brown Theological Institute and was originally located in Live Oak, Fla. The school was moved to Jacksonville in 1883 and renamed Edward Waters College.

In historic St. Augustine, the oldest continuously settled city in the United States, is Flagler College, a four-year private liberal arts college set in a beautiful campus of historic buildings such as the 1888 Spanish Renaissance-style Ponce de Leon Hotel commissioned by Standard Oil magnate, developer and philanthropist Henry M. Flagler. Flagler relishes its intimate, historic atmosphere with a limited enrollment of about 1,300.

For students interested in jobs in the business or legal professions, Jones College offers everything from court reporting and medical dictation to accounting. The college has a long history in the area, founded in 1918 by Annie Harper Jones for specialized business training. The main campus is in Arlington on the east bank of the St. Johns River, but the school also has a campus on the Westside (and a branch campus in Miami).

Mark McCumber

I was born in Jacksonville and grew up across the street from the 14th hole of a Donald Ross-designed municipal golf course. My brothers and I pulled weeds there for a quarter a bucket and golf privileges. I love Jacksonville, and except for a two-year absence to attend Brooklyn Bethel in New York, I've always lived here.

My own children were born here and I wanted them to grow up in the same area I did, enjoying the same great city. Jacksonville has more to offer its residents now than it ever has.

Naturally, one of my favorite things about Jacksonville and its surrounding areas is the abundance of noteworthy golf courses, public and private. I have enjoyed watching Jacksonville grow and seeing so many outstanding golf courses added to its landscape. It is especially gratifying to know that my company and family have played a role in this growth. After spending a majority of my life living on the west side of the city, my family and I have really enjoyed the last six years living near the ocean, another wonderful feature of this area.

Although I have traveled all over the world, I am always eager to come home. When I fly into Jacksonville International Airport and we start descending from 30,000 feet, I see the familiar sites of my hometown and realize that some of the most important events in my life and career have taken place in this city that I call home.

Mark McCumber is a PGA Tour Professional and president of his golf course design company, Mark McCumber & Associates.

As Jacksonville has grown, KPMG Peat Marwick has matched its pace. Today, Peat Marwick is the leading professional services firm in North Florida. It is known for its professional excellence, its dedication to quality client service and its active role in community affairs. For more than 50 years, the Jacksonville office of Peat Marwick and its predecessor firm has served as accountants, tax consultants and business advisors to many of the area's most successful companies and individuals. Peat Marwick's achievements over the years have been inextricably interwoven with Jacksonville's emergence as one of the leading financial, commercial and medical centers in the nation.

"At Peat Marwick," Managing Partner Larry J. Thoele explains, "our goal is to be the single best resource for solving the business problems of our clients. To achieve this goal, we are absolutely committed to delivering unsurpassed quality service. Our definition of quality includes serving our clients by understanding the industry within which they operate. Interdisciplinary industry teams composed of audit, tax and management consulting personnel focus on our clients' needs and serve the needs of specific industry markets."

Service delivery along industry lines has proven to be very successful for Peat Marwick. They serve a diverse clientele ranging from large publicly-held corporations, privately-owned businesses, entrepreneurs and individuals. These include retailers, manufacturers, financial institutions, insurance companies, health care providers, educational institutions, not-for-profit entities, transportation concerns and real estate companies. A significant segment of Peat Marwick's practice in Jacksonville is the small-to-medium-sized company. This entrepreneurial market reflects the majority of businesses throughout the First Coast and, in turn, underscores Peat Marwick's commitment to being the best resource to serve Jacksonville businesses.

As Florida's First Coast experiences the growing influence of world economic developments and international markets, Peat Marwick is uniquely positioned to help their clients capitalize on the opportunities of the thriving global economy. KPMG, recognized as a Global Leader, is the world's largest professional services firm with 1,100 offices in 125 countries. The fir-

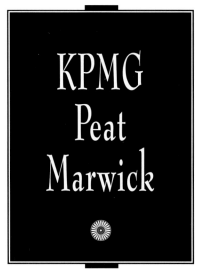

m's portfolio of special services is designed to help businesses of all sizes participate in the exciting growth opportunities that are developing around the world. For Jacksonville businesses, this translates into resources that are available at home — and around the globe.

"As one of the largest professional service organizations in Jacksonville, our strength has always been our people," states Thoele. "The abilities of our personnel are the measure by which our clients judge us. Recognizing this, we are committed to hiring only the most qualified professionals and then making a substantial investment in their career development. Our emphasis on quality people, coupled with superior training, is a proven formula that allows us to achieve professional excellence and a consistent delivery of outstanding service." With offices located in the Independent Life building, Peat Marwick professionals continue their tradition of providing quality service.

Peat Marwick's vision of quality commitment for their professionals extends beyond a well-developed inventory of technical and business advisory skills. Quality commitment means giving, too. Peat Marwick's professionals are encouraged to give their time, talents and financial resources back to the community in which they live. Non-profit organizations

Pete Marwick's Jacksonville partners are (from left, bottom row) James A. Heinz, Managing Partner Larry J. Thoele, Robert H. Lovic. (Left, top row) Steve F. Perez, Gary S. Whitmore, S. Mark Hand, Robert J. Wuggazer, Daniel R. Curran.

throughout Jacksonville — from charitable and civic associations to the Jacksonville Symphony and the University of North Florida — benefit from the significant involvement of Peat Marwick professionals who contribute to the quality of life found on Florida's First Coast.

Since the 1950s, Jacksonville's downtown skyline grew dramatically as new businesses came to town and established companies enlarged their offices. More recently, impressive suburban office complexes have sprouted on the city's Southside.

One company, Law Engineering, has been involved in most of Jacksonville's major building projects since it opened an office here in 1956. Law Engineering's role is to provide geotechnical engineering services — soil testing, evaluation and selection of foundation systems. Law's material testing and inspection services are an integral part of construction quality control.

Law Engineering's recent projects range from transportation projects like the Fuller Warren Bridge Replacement to suburban office building and manufacturing facilities like the Merrill Lynch and Vistakon developments in Deerwood Park.

With expanding and changing environmental regulations, businesses turn to Law Engineering for a wide variety of environmental consulting services such as site assessments, underground storage tank consulting, indoor air quality services, wetland surveys and lead-based paint testing. The company uses an engineering approach to help building facility managers cost effectively solve problems related to asbestos containing materials, roofing, paving and building materials.

Founded in Atlanta in 1946, Law Engineering has 30 branch offices around the country with five in the growing state of Florida. The employee-owned company has a staff of 1,900 nationwide with nearly 100 in Jacksonville. There are 30 experienced soils and materials engineers, 11 of whom are registered professionals. Serving clients from Savannah to Gainesville and as far west as Tallahassee, the Jacksonville office has two drill rigs and a complete laboratory for testing soil and construction materials.

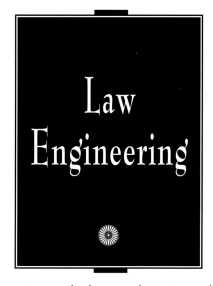

Law Engineering

"Northeast Florida continues to challenge our staff from both a technical and business point of view. Technically, unique soil conditions, complex environmental situations and construction material problem solving create opportunities for our staff," says James A. Horton, vice president and branch manager of the Jacksonville office. "The business climate also creates opportunties in all sectors: public, commercial and industrial. We look forward to a healthy 1990s."

Law Engineering

"Of all that exists, man is unique — he creates. What remains the same is the creative process — what changes are the tools by which he creates." So says the marketing brochure of Saxelbye Architects, Inc., a firm whose creativity goes back to the early part of the century, but whose tools are most current.

Englishman Harold Saxelbye came to Jacksonville in 1913 to help rebuild the city after the devastating fire of 1901. The architect was among a group of visionaries who helped the city blossom into a bold southern commercial and distribution center. Saxelbye designed a number of landmark Jacksonville buildings such as the signature Mayflower Hotel, the Cummer Gallery of Art, Epping Forest and was integral to the development of the historic San Jose neighborhood. About a dozen of his historic structures remain standing today, including the 1927-Levy Mercantile Building, now known as the Saxelbye Building, which serves as Saxelbye Architects' offices.

Saxelbye's firm continues to flourish today as the oldest practicing architectural firm in

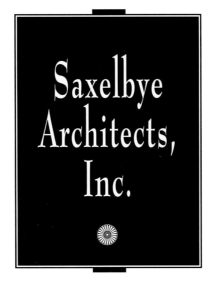

Florida and as one of the largest Florida-based architectural and interiors firms. The firm continues its tradition of playing a key role in the growth of Jacksonville with its involvement in recent major projects including BancBoston Mortgage Corporation's national headquarters, Blue Cross & Blue Shield of Florida's suburban campus, Gran Park at the Avenues, Ponte Vedra Surf Club, and the new Center for the Arts at Florida Community College of Jacksonville just to name a few.

Saxelbye's impressive projects are erected throughout the Southeast. The company recently finished Reichhold World Headquarters & Laboratories in Research Triangle Park, North Carolina. This project was the third largest corporate relocation in America in 1992. The diversity of the firm is best evidenced by a multitude of facility types including banks, corporate office buildings, computer centers, schools, churches, government buildings and historic preservation and renovations. Notable renovations include Union Terminal, Robert E. Lee High School, University of Florida Griffin-Floyd Hall and the Edward Ball Building. Saxelbye is currently restoring Henry Klutho's downtown St. James Building to serve as Jacksonville's City Hall.

While the firm handles a wide range of projects, it is noted for office design. The company has designed 43 office buildings over the past decade. With a unique propriety computerized component design system, "CDS^{TM}," Saxelbye can expedite the design of an office building in half the time of conventional design process. Saxelbye also uses their component design system for other types of projects such as banks, schools, post offices and industrial buildings. Another specialty is the firm's interior capabilities with a full-service interior design studio. Saxelbye has excelled in providing programming, space planning and interior design services for many

Saxelbye Architects, Inc.

clients including the 42-story Barnett Center, Computer Power, Inc., Crowley Maritime and AT&T, just to name a few.

One of the firm's greatest strengths in maintaining quality for the client from start to finish, is its studio structure. Under the studio system, employees are organized into teams rather than departments. "Instead of one company of 40 employees you really have seven smaller companies under one umbrella that allows us to be very responsive to our clients," says Larry Ponder, AIA, Saxelbye's president and principal owner. "Under the studio concept clients have the same team of specialists from day one until the day the client moves into the building. That allows for continuity and quality control."

Maintaining high standards of quality means focusing on the client's needs and opinions. Throughout the evolution of each project, clients have opportunities to evaluate the work and rate the services. In turn, Saxelbye takes the information to continually improve its performance.

The central philosophy at Saxelbye remains: "Listening to the client's expectations and concerns and responding within budgetary and time constraints."

Vistakon, Jacksonville's largest manufacturer, continues to grow in stature in Northeast Florida. A Johnson & Johnson company that develops, manufactures and distributes disposable contact lenses, Vistakon recently completed its fourth operations site in Jacksonville.

In the last four years, Vistakon has added over 1,000 jobs for a total of more than 1,600 employees.

Vistakon manufactures and markets the ACU-VUE® Disposable Contact Lens — the first disposable contact lens. ACUVUE® was test marketed in Jacksonville in 1987, then introduced nationwide in 1988. Now it is the number one selling disposable contact lens in the world. The pace of research and development continued. The next product launched by the company was SUREVUE®, the first daily wear lens that can be used for two weeks, then replaced with a fresh pair.

Recently Vistakon's latest advancement in disposable contact lenses was released. 1-DAY ACUVUE® is a disposable lens worn for just one day then discarded and replaced with a new pair the next day.

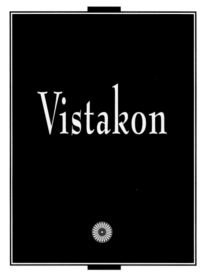

Vistakon spends hundreds of millions of dollars to advance its technology and provide people with the safest, most comfortable disposable lenses.

"All of our worldwide research and manufacturing operations are located in Jacksonville," said Vistakon President Bernard W. Walsh. "And one of the major contributing factors to our success has been the availability of a terrific work force here in Jacksonville — which was a key reason we decided to expand locally."

The company's standing in Northeast Florida cannot be overstated. Vistakon is important to the local community both because it represents high-technology medical manufacturing and its reputation as a quality employer with progressive human resources policies.

Vistakon is committed to supporting the Jacksonville community through good works and charitable contributions. Vistakon has been actively involved in United Way at Work, Junior Achievement, public television's WJCT TV 7, INROADS, Duval County Board of Education Partnership Program and the Jacksonville Collaborative Child Care Consortium. Additionally, Vistakon donated

more than $900,000 to the United Way of Northeast Florida. Many of Vistakon's employees are active civic volunteers and many others serve on the Board of Directors of area non-profit organizations.

Johnson & Johnson, the largest and most diversified organization in the medical field, moved into Jacksonville and the contact lens business in 1981 when it purchased Frontier Contact Lens of Florida. A year after the firm was purchased, the name was changed to Vistakon and its growth in the community has continued at a rapid pace. Following Johnson & Johnson's philosophy of making major contributions to the medical world and striving to become the best in their field, Vistakon immediately undertook state-of-the-art research and development activities that resulted in the development of the disposable lens.

Vistakon operates from four sites throughout Jacksonville. A new $50-million Deerwood Park facility was recently completed to expand the company's manufacturing, research and development operations. Another facility in Deerwood serves as the hub for distribution. Administrative offices are located in Southpoint and another manufacturing operation is located on Richard Street.

Leading Vistakon is president Bernard W. Walsh, a longtime Johnson & Johnson executive. Employees of the company come from a vast number of professions and trades, including chemists, biologists, engineers and a broad range of manufacturing technologists. The company uses a team approach in tackling its problems and setting goals. Representatives from all levels of the firm, from upper management to line workers, meet together regularly to address issues and involve employees in the decision-making process.

In the last decade, Jacksonville has established itself as a healthcare cluster, including a center for medical manufacturing. Vistakon has been at the center of that development, making growing commitments to the region.

Jacksonville was founded at a narrow crossing along the mighty St. Johns River. Discovered originally by Native American Indians, this land was Spanish, French and English colonial property in the 17th, 18th and early 19th centuries.

Permanent settlement of this land took place in the early 1800s as Florida became a territory of the fledgling United States of America. Originally known as Cow Ford, Jacksonville was renamed in the 1820s to honor President Andrew Jackson who was once provisional territorial governor of Florida.

Jacksonville continued to grow throughout the 19th and early 20th centuries, despite two devastating fires and the Civil War. Beginning with World War I, Jacksonville became a transportation hub with its deep-water port and extensive railway connections. The city became known as the "Gateway to Florida."

Today, Jacksonville is a key transportation hub for the southeastern United States. Jacksonville is also home for many banking, insurance and investment headquarters. Jacksonville provides an inviting climate in weather and business.

The city is also enjoying a rebirth through the River City Renaissance; a plan to rejuvenate Jacksonville's public parks, auditoriums and arenas to stimulate private business growth and create new jobs.

Northeast Florida, from Amelia Island to St. Augustine, provides many natural amenities. Mild weather, sun-drenched beaches, and beautiful rivers make up a setting that is second to none. The people in this region enjoy a quality of life filled with golf, tennis, water sports, concerts, museums, parks and festivals.

Jacksonville is the home of the Gator Bowl Classic college football game, The Players Championship golf tournament, the Amelia Island women's tennis tournament, the Jacksonville Jazz Festival, and many other nationally known events.

Northeast Florida also serves as the headquarters for the Professional Golf Association (PGA) and the Association of Tennis Professionals (ATP). The city is also regional headquarters for American Express, Merrill Lynch, Vistakon (a division of Johnson & Johnson), American Tourister, AT&T Universal Card and AT&T American Transtech among many others.

More than 14 million people drive through Jacksonville annually along Interstate 95. Jacksonville is served by 27 non-stop flights daily from throughout the southeastern and midwestern United States.

Jacksonville offers many incentives for business relocation, including Enterprise Zone benefits, Tax Increment Financing, land assembly, tax abatement, and many others. The city's unique consolidated city-county government helps expedite services for its citizens.

Florida's First Coast, Duval County and Jacksonville are names representing an area of rich history, consistent growth, friendly business atmosphere, and an incomparable quality of life.

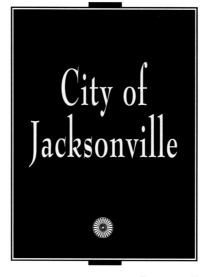

City of Jacksonville

The ever-expanding Scott-McRae Group began August 7, 1916, when Ford Motor Company made the official appointment of Duval Motor Company, now Duval Ford, as a dealer. Since then, Duval Ford has been outstandingly successful as an automobile dealership dedicated to community service. Duval Ford is the "flagship" of the Scott-McRae Group. Scott-McRae Group is a diversified operating/holding company engaged in the management and ownership of innovative, dynamic and profitable companies throughout Florida and the Southeast. Its mission is to provide superior services and products to its customers in every area of business; engage in the fair management of quality people and provide them with fulfilling career opportunities; represent, effectively and fairly, the business for which it has agreed to provide services and products in its assigned market areas and to support the local communities by being a good corporate citizen.

The Scott-McRae Group subsidiaries include: Duval Ford, Duval Honda, Duval Acura, Tampa Hondaland, Gatorland Toyota, U.S. Auto Credit, Autolease Corporation of Florida, All Fleet, Scott-McRae Advertising, Scott-McRae Properties, Spectrum Services, Automotive Management Services and newly acquired Brandon Honda and Duval Collision Center.

Henry H. "Tip" Graham, President and CEO
Scott-McRae Group

More than 77 years ago Duval Ford was located in downtown Jacksonville at the corner of Lee and Forsyth streets and remained there for more than 50 years. Finally, in March 1968, the company officially opened its current location at 1616 Cassat Avenue. In new car sales Duval Ford is the 74th largest Ford dealership in the nation and is currently ranked first in leasing in Florida.

Duval Honda in Jacksonville was the second Honda franchise in Florida and among the first 100 in the nation. This new line of imports grew rapidly and expansion was necessary to its present location at 1290 Cassat Avenue. Duval Honda continues to win awards in vehicle sales, parts and service.

The Scott-McRae Group opened the doors of Duval Acura on Atlantic Boulevard at Regency Square in March 1986, establishing one of the first Acura deal-

erships in Florida and the 24th in the United States. Since then, award-winning Duval Acura has become a first-rank dealership and a recognized member of the Jacksonville community.

Tampa Hondaland, located in Tampa, Fla., is the second largest Honda dealer in Florida and ranks as the 17th largest Honda dealer in the United States. The most recent automotive acquisitions enlarging the Scott-McRae Group include Gatorland Toyota in Gainesville and Brandon Honda in Tampa.

Scott-McRae's Autolease firm, with its large fleet, has been in operation since 1952. All Fleet, located at Duval Ford, provides small and large fleets of cars to an expanding list of customers. Spectrum Services was formed to support automotive companies, fleet operators and individual owners by preparing vehicles for sale and/or private use and has been serving customers since 1985. Automotive Management Services was established in March 1991 as a division of the Scott-McRae Group dedicated to providing detailed training in the principles and management of franchise dealer financing or Buy Here Pay Here. Auto Credit of Florida, a subsidiary of U.S. Auto Credit, finances vehicles sold by dealerships owned by the Scott-McRae Automotive Group Inc. and by dealers who are in a joint venture or management agreement with the U.S. Auto Credit and its subsidiaries. These dealerships currently include the six Scott-McRae dealerships, three Atlanta dealerships and one Jacksonville dealer.

Outside the automobile industry, there is Scott-McRae Advertising and Scott-McRae Properties, a real estate firm. Operating for more than 26 years, the advertising agency provides advertising services for automotive clients and additionally serves a diverse group of clients. The real estate company was founded in 1985 to coordinate existing properties for future dealerships and investments such as the new Riverside Center executive offices.

First Union National Bank of Florida, headquartered in Jacksonville, is the city's largest bank and the second largest bank in the state. The Florida-based bank is part of First Union Corporation which is headquartered in Charlotte, N.C., and operates as one of the largest banks in the nation with more than $71 billion in assets.

With nearly 50 branches in the First Coast market and nearly 500 branches statewide, First Union is conveniently located to most of the state's expansive population.

First Union National Bank of Florida traces its origins to Atlantic Bancorporation, founded in Jacksonville in 1903. First Union really took off following a 1985 federal court ruling that paved the way for interstate banking.

In November of that same year, the $3.8 billion-asset Atlantic Bancorporation was acquired by Charlotte's First Union Corp. Through an impressive series of further acquisitions, First Union has grown into the second largest bank in Florida with $28 billion in assets.

One of the biggest deals was the acquisition of $7.8 billion Jacksonville-based Florida National Bank, completed in January of 1990. In September, 1991, First Union was chosen by banking regulators to takeover the then financially-troubled $11.2 billion Miami-based Southeast Bank in a deal assisted by the FDIC.

Beyond the traditional banking services, First Union offers customized products to fit individual needs. Some of these services include customized banking programs which offer a special checking account with added convenient money-saving features. They also offer savings accounts, certificates of deposit, money market accounts, individual retirement accounts, credit cards, home mortgages and tax-advantage loans.

Often times, customers may have needs for more than traditional banking services. To meet this need, First Union offers a full line of invest-

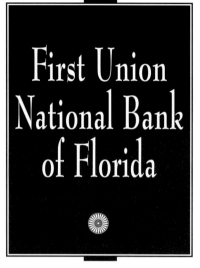

ment services including mutual funds, brokerage services, an asset management account and personal trust services.

For First Union business customers, a wide range of commercial checking, commercial savings and commercial money market investment accounts are available. Commerical lending, cash management services and international banking are also part of this business-customer focus.

But offering customized services and convenient locations is only as good as the service behind it. That's why First Union has an extensive program of training and monitoring the customer service behaviors of its employees. First Union employees are "shopped" to be sure they extend this quality customer service. Customers are surveyed to monitor their opinions and their experiences concerning First Union's service. From this information, services and processes are changed and enhanced to offer the best quality service.

This philosophy of service is even extended to First Union's advertising. With every ad displaying the tag line: "When it comes to service, everything matters," the commitment to personal service is reinforced to each customer and employee.

First Union is an active community supporter and is involved in many of Jacksonville's events. Some of these events include The Players Championship golf tournament, the Jacksonville Jazz Festival, the Ortega River Run, the St. Johns River City Band and Jacksonville University athletics.

First Union also supports Jacksonville development by supporting projects like the Chamber of Commerce's Cornerstone project and membership drives and the National Football League expansion program.

With the belief that investing in the communities they serve is good business for everyone, First Union continues to be a community leader not only in Jacksonville but in the state and regions in which it operates.

As bright orange beams dance through the downtown traffic and the quiet power of the St. Johns River rushes past its feet, the Gulf Life Tower stands tall, dominating Jacksonville's Southbank as it has for more than 25 years. Perched high above the city on the Tower's 27th floor, the University Club embraces a bird's eye view that truly reflects the essence of Jacksonville and the University Club itself.

Established in 1968, the University Club was founded by Stanley Nichaus and a handful of local businessmen who had one purpose in mind.

"The University Club has been conceived, designed and originated to set a new standard of excellence for the Jacksonville area and the Southeast. Each facet of the Club — Membership, food, drink and service — has been carefully planned to secure the needs and enjoyment of its Membership."

And for 25 years, the University Club has discreetly and distinctively done just that.

Since its inception, the University Club has been on the cutting edge of Jacksonville's business and social scene. Lunchtime crowds regularly draw prominent business men and women, and city officials to table-top drawing boards where new ideas and deal closings happen over fine wine and chateaubriand.

By nightfall the business day is done and the evening crowd emerges only to lose themselves in the luxury of fine dining and unmatched service. Inside this prestigious establishment special accommodations know no limits. Whether the choice is traditional dining, a privately catered gathering or a romantic evening for

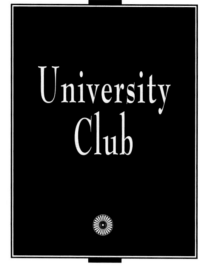

two in a private dining room, no detail is overlooked.

Adding to the charm of the University Club is its one-of-a-kind 18th century decor. Dark mahogany walls, some of which were once part of an old English castle, and original 18th century antiques reflect the Club's formal, yet comfortable ambiance.

In unique contrast to the University Club's masculine stature, the impeccable yet gracious service staff combines intimate rapport with traditional southern hospitality to create an impressively personalized experience. Each guest is not only known by name but by their individual needs. From domed covered plates served in precise unison to favorite after dinner cordials that need no requesting, guests find themselves relaxed and pampered in their home away from home.

Guests can enjoy their "home away from home" no matter where business or personal matters may take them. Whether it's a golfing get-a-way weekend at Pinehurst, North Carolina; an intense business meeting at the Tower Club in Fort Lauderdale; or a trip abroad to the St. James in Paris, there are more than 170 Associate Clubs located worldwide to continue the traditions of the University Club.

As the University Club continues to look down upon a city of change, it remains a steadfast embodiment of the community below. By setting new standards and continually striving for excellence, the University Club not only plays an integral role in the Jacksonville of today, but provides an enduring cornerstone to building the Jacksonville of tomorrow.

In 1953, Jacksonville's reputation as an insurance center took a big leap forward with Prudential's decision to establish one of its regional offices in the city. Prudential was completing a dramatic decentralization process to move operations closer to policyholders and chose Jacksonville as its South-Central Home Office over a number of other southern cities such as Atlanta, Birmingham, Charlotte, Knoxville, Nashville and Richmond.

When Prudential completed its riverfront office tower in 1955, it was the tallest building in Florida. The company continued to build its presence in Jacksonville, finding a quality labor market, a pleasant climate and a growing transportation hub in the emerging city. In 1985, a second impressive complex, Prudential's Operations Center, was added to Jacksonville's south-bank skyline.

Today, Prudential is one of the largest and most diversified financial organizations in the world. The 100,000-employee international company offers a myriad of insurance and health-care management products, bro-

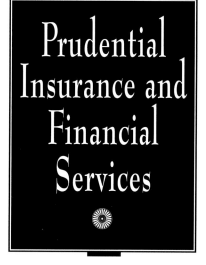

Prudential Insurance and Financial Services

kerage and mortgage services and financial instruments. The company's size, cash flow and asset management expertise make it one of the world's largest investors. Though a huge corporation, Prudential's goal remains to help each of its customers achieve financial security and peace of mind.

The Greater Southern Operations of Prudential Insurance and Financial Services in Jacksonville serves people from Cleveland to Key West and west to El Paso, Texas. Forty-one sales offices throughout Florida serve policyholders. To get a sense of Prudential's impact in the Sunshine state, just consider that in 1991 Prudential had almost $33 billion of life insurance in force in Florida and real estate investments of more than $2 billion.

Prudential is a major employer in Northeast Florida, providing almost 5,000 jobs in the region to workers who enjoy strong salary and benefit plans. In fact, Prudential has one of the most comprehensive benefits packages in American business.

Since moving to Jacksonville, Prudential has been committed to contributing to the quality of life. Associates volunteer thousands of hours in community service each year and in 1992 established the Employee Outreach Committee so that Prudential employees could best target their efforts to the needs of the community. The company has traditionally been among the top contributors to United Way and other worthy causes. In 1992, Florida's Commissioner of Education recognized Prudential's "outstanding support of education."

The Prudential's core values have helped it continue to flourish in the marketplace: Worthy of Trust, Customer Focused, Respect for Each Other and Winning. Those values guide Prudential in all its dealings with its clients, its associates and the communities in which it operates.

Prudential Insurance and Financial Services

The roots of CSX Transportation are intertwined with the roots of Jacksonville.

Today, Jacksonville is headquarters to CSX Transportation, one of the nation's largest railroads, and a direct descendant of the oldest railroad in America, the Baltimore & Ohio, which was chartered as the first common carrier railroad in 1827.

CSX Transportation presently has some 5,000 employees in Jacksonville in a wide variety of occupations from headquarters staff to locomotive engineers to track workers to computer programmers. CSXT is a unit of CSX Corporation, an international transportation company with revenues of more than $8.5 billion, headquartered in Richmond, Virginia.

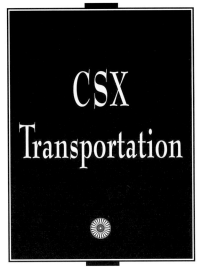

Railroad employees are involved in every aspect of the cultural, civic, business and political life of Jacksonville. Indeed, the partnership of the railroad and city takes many shapes, including such landmarks as the rail passenger station now known as the Prime Osborn Convention Center, named for the late Prime S. Osborn III, the first chairman of CSX Corporation and a Jacksonville civic leader for many years. In every way, CSX is committed to the city. In fact, CSX investment in Jacksonville in the past several years alone has exceeded $100 million.

The railroad of today is a legacy of the city's first rails laid in the 1850s. The fledging Florida, Atlantic & Gulf Central is notable for, among other things, being financed by the first bonds issued by the city. After a couple of fitful starts by other companies, Dr. Abel Seymour Baldwin laid

Dispatchers at Operations Center on Warrington Street control some 1,300 trains a day. (CSX Transportation)

rails in Jacksonville and extended them in 1857 to Alligator, later to become Lake City. Meanwhile, U.S. Sen. David L. Yulee started the Florida Railroad, from Fernandina to Cedar Key. All of these lines today are part of CSX.

Through the years, rails linked Jacksonville with development across the state and the growing industrial might of the country. However, the city didn't emerge as a major railroad headquarters city until the late 1950s, when the Atlantic Coast Line Railroad, which had outgrown its headquarters in Wilmington, N.C., started looking for a new home.

Jacksonville was one of several southern cities under consideration, but with a well-organized effort from the business and political communities, Jacksonville won out.

In 1958, ACL began construction of its new headquarters building on the St. Johns River. In July 1960, ACL completed its move of 950 employees and their families and officially opened the new building. In 1967, the building became headquarters for the newly merged ACL and Seaboard Air Line Railroad, which together became Seaboard Coast Line Railroad.

In 1980, Seaboard Coast Line merged with the Chessie System Railroads, encompassing the B&O and Chesapeake & Ohio, to form CSX Corporation. CSX Transportation was the business unit formed in 1986 to operate the combined railroads, initially with headquarters in Jacksonville, Cleveland and Baltimore. By 1992, all headquarters functions of the railroad were relocated in Jacksonville.

Today, CSX Transportation provides rail service over more than 18,000 route miles to 20 states, Washington, D.C., and Ontario, Canada. In Jacksonville, major customers include Seminole Kraft, Anheuser Busch, Maxwell House, Jefferson-Smurfit, Jacksonville Electric Authority, SCM-Glidden, Owens Corning and the Jacksonville Port Authority.

Among the company's largest business markets are automobiles, chemicals, forest products, coal and phosphate. In fact, CSXT hauls more coal and phosphate than any other railroad. In West Virginia and Kentucky, the railroad serves many of the mines that produce the lowest sulfur coal in the east, especially important in these environmentally-conscious times.

Phosphate originates in the Bone Valley region in west central Florida. Mines scattered through the region provide phosphate and fertilizers to the nation's bread basket and, from ports on Tampa Bay, to international agricultural producers.

In addition to the landmark downtown headquarters on the North Bank, installations vital to the railroad are found on the Westside and the Southside.

On the Westside is the nerve center of railroad operations, the Transportation Center. The center houses all the dispatching and locomotive management operations that were scattered across the eastern U.S. before the mergers. From the center, some 1,300 trains a day are dispatched, making CSXT the first U.S. railroad to control its core trackage from one location.

On Jacksonville's Southside is the Customer Service Center, the hub for customer service activities.

CSXT transports coal vital to many of Florida's utilities, including the JEA.

The CSC also has benefitted from centralized operations in Jacksonville. It is from this facility in the Southpoint office complex that customers place orders for railroad cars and receive shipping information and billing. Some 12,000 customer telephone calls are handled each day by the employees at the center.

As the result of these consolidation projects and the relocation of all railroad headquarters activities to Jacksonville, hundreds of employees have moved to the city in recent years.

Also at Southpoint is the Advanced Information Technology Center, the hub for the railroad's computer operations. This fail-safe, weather-proof structure was designed to withstand anything nature could throw at it, including hurricanes and power outages. It is here that main-frame computers drive customer information functions.

To this day, Jacksonville is an important hub for rail traffic with CSXT's Moncrief Yard on the Westside linking Jacksonville's industries to suppliers and customers. The switching yard at Baldwin, a few miles west of downtown, also connects South Florida with the rest of the country.

Intermodal movements — still known colloquially as piggyback — are an increasingly important service for customers who rely on timely movement of goods from door to door. The truck-to-rail facility of sister company CSX Intermodal, also on the West Side, provides prompt service to customers in Jacksonville, the Southeast and across the country.

The railroad also is the primary connection for the Port of Jacksonville, both at Blount Island and at the Tallyrand Docks and Terminals. Another CSX sister company, Sea-Land Service Inc., also serves Blount Island and connects Jacksonville's powerhouse transportation network with the world.

CSXT, the people who move Jacksonville, are proud to be a part of a city on the move.

CSXT's landmark headquarters building on Jacksonville's downtown waterfront.

111

Barnett Bank of Jacksonville, N.A., founded in 1877, is the city's only "hometown" bank that continues today as a major financial institution. Additionally, the bank's parent company, Barnett Banks, Inc., and eight affiliated support companies are headquartered in Jacksonville, giving Barnett a prominent role in shaping the area's economy and quality of life.

The Barnett legacy was begun in Jacksonville by Willam Boyd Barnett and his son Bion in a small banking room within the Freedman's Bank Building on Main Street. The Barnett banking tradition continues today from company headquarters a short block away in the 42-story Barnett Center, the tallest structure on Jacksonville's downtown skyline, and from auxillary operations at the 102-acre Barnett Office Park south of downtown.

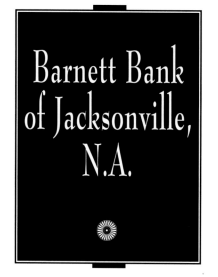

The modern Barnett Bank of Jacksonville is a $2.4 billion asset institution with more than 30 branch locations throughout the metropolitan Jacksonville area. The bank, under the direction of chief executive officer and president Andy Cheney, takes the lead in addressing the business, civic, and philanthropic needs of the Jacksonville community. Barnett's reputation as a socially responsible corporate citizen dates to the bank's earliest years when founders helped the Jacksonville community weather economic hardships, natural disasters of freeze and fire, and a deadly plague of yellow fever. In fact, the bank played a vital role in Jacksonville's recovery following its greatest natural disaster, the 1901 fire. The bank building was the only financial institution to survive the fire and became the community's repository for cash and valuables during post-fire reconstruction.

Barnett's community commitment is evidenced today by the volunteer work of bank officers with the chamber of commerce, the United Way, local government commissions, area civic clubs, and non-profit organizations in education, human service, health and the arts. Additionally, the bank's employee volunteer program, recognized in January 1993 as the 1012 "Point of Light" by former President George Bush, establishes partnerships between bank units and area non-profit agencies. These outreach efforts collectively provide more than 60,000 volunteer hours each year toward community needs.

Barnett also initiates major projects to address specific community concerns. One example is the

bank's award-winning partnership with Matthew Gilbert Middle School. To ensure the success of Gilbert's magnet program in finance, Barnett established in 1991 a student-run bank within the school building through the donation of in-kind services and equipment valued at approximately $17,000 and more than 1,000 hours of volunteer time. Another effort in the field of education was the creation of the Barnett Institute at the University of North Florida. This interdisciplinary institute is dedicated to solving practical problems in business and was established with a multi-year grant of more than $680,000.

Housing issues are also a major area for community outreach. To assist public housing residents in becoming homeowners, Barnett partnered with the Jesse Ball duPont Fund to finance and develop "Moving Up Housing." The two-year program involves the city, the state, the Urban League, and the National Council of Negro Women in transitioning participants toward financial independence. Barnett was also the first corporation to sponsor Habitat for Humanity's "House Raising Week" in Jacksonville. Every year since 1989, Barnett has funded construction of one or more homes and sent volunteers to work beside families building their Habitat homes. Additionally, Barnett created a special program, H.O.M.E., to offer discounted mortgage rates and special terms for low-income residents seeking to buy a home.

Economic development is another Barnett concern. The bank established an innovative program at the University of North Florida Small Business Development Center. The effort, "Thinking B.I.G.," is a business "incubator without walls" that provides individual counseling and direct management assistance to help promising small businesses accelerate their rate of growth. Barnett was also an initial corporate investor in the Jacksonville Chamber of Commerce Cornerstone initiative for economic and community development.

Barnett's own impact on the Jacksonville economy is generated by substantial real estate holdings and a combined workforce of more than 5,000 people receiving income in excess of $131.5 million. The Barnett companies rank among the top 10 area employers, according to the *Jacksonville Business Journal*.

The company's signature downtown building, The Barnett Center, leads the group of area real estate holdings. Barnett Center opened in July 1990 as northeast Florida's tallest structure with approximately 656,000 square feet of office space. Barnett Banks Inc. and the Barnett Bank of Jacksonville together occupy 14 of the building's 42 floors. Twenty additional tenants bring a large additional workforce to the downtown area. The Barnett

Center houses a grand banking lobby, an 8,000 square-foot YMCA Fitness Center, and parking for more than 650 vehicles. Barnett's suburban campus complex, the Barnett Office Park, contains 1.3 million square feet in 11 buildings. It opened in 1989 to house Barnett's non-banking affiliates: Barnett Banks Trust Company, Barnett Technologies, Barnett Recovery Corporation, Barnett Securities Inc., Barnett Insurance Company, Barnett Mortgage Company and Barnett Card Services Corporation.

More than 3,000 employees work in the setting which houses an innovative multi-purpose facility complete with an employee cafeteria, a YMCA Fitness Center, 25 training/conference rooms, a state-of-the-art media center and video production facility, and a branch bank that often serves as a testing ground for new technology and services. The campus also includes a 20,000 square-foot child development center that serves 366 pre-school children of employees. An on-site early learning center, operated in conjunction with the Duval County Public School System, opened in 1992, the first in the district. It offered a kindergarten and first grade program for the 1992-93 academic year and will ultimately offer a curriculum for children from kindergarten through the second grade.

Barnett's commitment to Jacksonville, begun more than a century ago, continues firm. The company's mission to be the preferred financial institution and employer in northeast Florida acknowledges its determination to fuel the continued development of this community.

Gate Petroleum Company, one of Jacksonville's most dynamic and diversified businesses, has always been an influential element in the growth of Northeast Florida. The multi-million dollar conglomerate started with a single gasoline station on Jacksonville's Northside in 1960. During the next three decades as the city grew in sweeping strides, so too did Gate Petroleum — supporting and thriving on the region's momentum.

Now, Gate Petroleum's business enterprises extend across a disparate field of operations that include 150 service stations and convenience stores in nine states, construction material manufacturing, building and renovation operations, maritime operations, elegant resorts and a powerful real estate division that includes one of Jacksonville's premier office parks and other property for future business development.

"Our business has continued to grow every year," says Don Davis, vice president of corporate relations.

Aggressive expansion into other areas of business continues. Gate's most recent addition is Gate Pallet Systems, an Indiana manufacturer of recyclable shipping pallets. Throughout the years Gate has provided fuel for Northeast Florida's businesses and residents, construction materials for its bridges and buildings, utilities for its homes, offices and residential communities for its workforce, port facilities for its maritime industry and luxurious resorts for its members and guests. And, Gate remains a strong corporate citizen. This summer, Gate helped lead the effort to bring an NFL expansion team to Jacksonville. The company was instrumental in bringing the prestigious Mayo Clinic satellite to Jacksonville in the 1980s. For years, Gate has been the

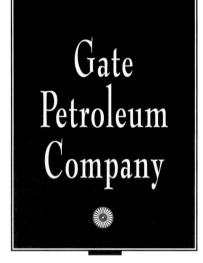

leading sponsor of the internationally-recognized 15 kilometer River Run, and has contributed to the development of the Ronald McDonald House, Wolfson Children's Hospital, and the Alzheimers Disease Control Center. Those are just a few of the hundreds of community and charitable causes Gate has supported.

The closely-held private corporation runs a little differently than typical large companies. Founder and President Herb Peyton surrounds himself with a small group of key executives who huddle regularly in early morning meetings. An extended family, Peyton credits the dedication of employees for the impressive growth of the company. "It has always been my belief that the value of a company can best be measured by its people rather than by its balance sheet," Peyton says.

The company's motto: "From can to can't." "It means you go from daybreak until you can't go anymore if that's what it takes," Davis explains.

In 1960, Peyton pumped gas and washed windows at his first service station at 45th Street and Moncrief Road in Jacksonville. By 1967 he had 28 full-service stations and that same year he branched out of Florida with a station in South Carolina.

During the 1970s, the convenience store became the logical partner for the corner service station. The first Gate convenience store opened in 1971, selling products easily consumed on the road.

Gate's first diversification from service station and convenience store operations came in 1974 with the purchase of a potato farm in the northeast Florida town of Hastings. Gate's agriculture division operated a 500-acre farm producing millions of pounds of potatoes each year until the farm was sold in 1990.

Gate Petroleum Company

Gate continued to diversify. Construction of Bigtree Racquet Club began in 1977, and in 1979 Gate Roofing Manufacturing Inc. began producing roll roofing felt. Now it's the largest such manufacturer under one roof in the country.

In 1981, the purchase of concrete plants in Texas, Alabama, and Florida led to the formation of Gate Concrete Products Division. During the 1980s, Gate renovated and modernized its service stations and convenience stores and for the past several years the company has continued to acquire prime locations and build new stations and stores.

In 1983, in one of the largest land deals in Florida, Gate bought the real estate holdings of Stockton, Whatley, Davin & Company and thus acquired thousands of acres of strategically located undeveloped property and took over the Ponte Vedra Inn & Club ocean front resort and the prestigious residential and recreational community of Deerwood.

The company's holdings expanded with the purchase of the Alfred I. DuPont estate and the development of Epping Forest Yacht Club and its adjacent luxury residential community. The company also developed Old Ponte Vedra Beach, an oceanfront condominium project and Blount Island, a maritime industrial complex which now houses the U.S. Marines ships prepositioning program.

No doubt Gate's diversified holdings will continue to grow. "We look for prospective acquisitions all the time," Davis says. "There is no telling what we might be doing a year from now."

Jacksonville is a city that is undeniably on the move; nothing new for this Northeast Florida community. Jacksonville's standard mode of operation is to address both opportunities and problems with vigor.

The community has a long proud history of removing barriers that might slow its forward motion. That was the reason for the founding of the Jacksonville Board of Trade back in 1884. When local business leaders found that silt was hindering commercial traffic on the St. Johns River, they banded together to dredge the channel and protect community interests.

That same entrepreneurial spirit was evident 42 years later when the organization, by then renamed the Jacksonville Chamber of Commerce, launched the nation's first community business promotion campaign. Called "Believers in Jacksonville," the media blitz touted the benefits of conducting business here with such headlines as "This all-year Florida city offers to many America's greatest opportunity to succeed."

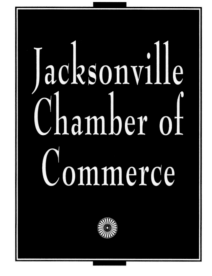

Jacksonville Chamber of Commerce

Today, Jacksonville continues to offer competitive advantages, and the Chamber remains an advocate for growth and positive change. The Chamber acts as a unified voice for the business community to both enhance the climate for commerce and to help attract new corporate citizens.

Recognizing that a leading factor in business relocation is the quality of the local workforce, the Chamber created a partnership in 1991 with the United Way of Northeast Florida, CSX Transportation, Winn Dixie and other local companies to address the issue. A similar effort to counter drug and alcohol abuse in the workplace was launched by the Chamber in 1989 and has helped over a hundred local companies become self-certified as drug-free, providing safety and peace of mind for thousands of employees and customers.

The Chamber has also initiated programs aimed at enhancing the bottom line of member businesses. In addition to activities and business-related educational semi-

Photo by Amy Calfee

nars and workshops, Chamber members have access to a health insurance program designed to meet the needs of smaller businesses.

In 1992, the Chamber created an innovative program called GO! (Growth and Opportunity) to help local businesses identify local expenditures and direct more dollars to local small woman- and minority-owned businesses. The effort now has over 100 participants which together have re-directed over $20 million to Jacksonville businesses.

The Chamber is an active participant in shaping the future of the community; it is an organization with a history of making a positive difference.

Baita International Inc. was founded in 1984 to assist foreign individuals and institutions wishing to participate as equity partners in commercial real estate projects in the United States. Headquartered in Jacksonville, the company represents Swiss, German and Dutch investment groups with offices in Germany and Switzerland for on-location service to those markets. Baita's primary business focus is the development, redevelopment and management of retail properties. It also provides management services for other commercial properties.

Acting in a fiduciary role, Baita develops the specific goals and strategies to secure the best possible real estate investment for its equity partners. One of the company's acquisition strategies is to purchase under-performing properties with value creation potential. Baita's expertise in choosing the proper strategies is proven. Under the company's management, turnaround has been achieved in numerous large retail centers, resulting in profitable renascence of these properties.

Baita's business strategy also targets exceptional development properties. The company is constantly investigating diverse types of real estate opportunities in ever-widening geographic areas when such markets offer attractive investment promise. Baita's goal is to have its finger on the pulse of thriving and emerging real estate markets throughout the southern states, a commitment that is consistently successful for its investment partners.

A recognized industry leader, Baita's substantial growth reflects the confidence and participation of international investors in Baita projects. Investment volume has grown from $6 million at the company's inception to nearly $300 million in 1993. And growth in leased square footage of owned and/or managed properties has climbed to close to 4 million square feet in 1993. The company ranks 26th on Monitor Magazine's listing of the top buyers of American retail property (Monitor's 22nd Annual Top 50 in Acquisition, January 1993 issue).

Baita offers competence in people and practices. The company's knowledgeable senior management has nearly 75 years of combined experience in the commercial

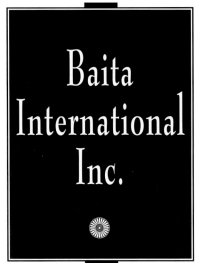

Reto J. Schneider, President and Chief Executive Officer.

The Park at Deerwood, Baita's Jacksonville Headquarters.

real estate industry, spanning several continents. Its highly-skilled and well-trained team of professionals provides the capability of identifying and capitalizing on carefully selected real estate opportunities. Team members are qualified in fields crucial to the proper analysis, acquisition, development, leasing, management and final disposition of real estate projects.

The company's two subsidiaries, Baita Property Services, Inc. and Baita Realty, Inc., provide a full range of professional management and leasing services to assure that foreign investors and U.S.-based owners receive all services necessary to maximize the potential from their real estate investments.

Baita Property Services, Inc., Baita's property management subsidiary, currently manages commercial properties totaling 3.5 million square feet, with 1 million of that total in third-party properties. With a hands-on management philosophy, Baita maintains offices in Orlando, Pensacola and Atlanta in addition to its professional staff in its Jacksonville headquarters.

Baita Realty, Inc., is the commercial real estate leasing and brokerage arm for Baita International and offers expertise to maximize the leasing potential of both Baita-owned and fee-managed properties. It is characterized by strong relationships with national and regional tenants and has worked successfully with members of the brokerage community in each of the Baita markets.

Baita takes pride in its ability to tailor projects to the specific needs and expectations of the individual investor. A successful acquisition, even within a growth-intensive area, poses an exacting challenge. To meet that challenge, Baita allocates the highest priority to analysis of financial, operational, demographic and other critical features to ensure equity partners outstanding market potential. The company now owns a total of 19 shopping centers and office buildings in Florida, Georgia, South Carolina and Alabama.

Emerging from one of the nation's most difficult recessionary periods with an expanding portfolio of properties, Baita is achieving great respect and visibility in the marketplace. A special combination of competence and commitment are the essentials for this

Riverplace, a Baita acquisition located in Jacksonville's affluent Mandarin area.

success and generate the momentum Baita will carry forward into the future.

President and founder, Reto J. Schneider, has a single-minded vision for Baita International: To become one of the major players in the development, redevelopment and management of retail properties in the United States.

Schneider and his wife, along with their Swiss-based partner Dr. Peter Bratschi, started the company 10 years ago from a small office in their home. Nine months later they moved into an office in Jacksonville's growing Baymeadows business district. Now they have 26 employees and offices in four cities in the Southeast and representative offices in Switzerland and Germany.

With a doctorate in economics, Schneider has guided real estate ventures throughout the world. For several years he was in Latin America and the Caribbean, involved in luxury resort developments. Then, Schneider went back to Europe where he also was involved in resort projects. From there, Schneider branched out and was the chief executive officer at a large general contracting firm doing business in the Middle East and West Africa. He was in Iran when the Khomeini-led revolution forced the company out.

While Schneider has worked throughout the world, he chose Jacksonville for his international company. Traditionally, companies

such as Baita are found in more cosmopolitan, international cities, Schneider says. But the company has flourished in Jacksonville and become a strong asset to Northeast Florida, bringing in clients from around the world. When Baita's competition was focused mostly on cities like New York, Dallas, Houston and Los Angeles, cities such as Jacksonville, Tampa and Charlotte were neglected. But Schneider was accurate in predicting that the Southeast was poised for tremendous growth.

Richland Fashion Mall in Columbia, South Carolina, was Baita's largest acquisition.

BancBoston Mortgage Corporation's impact is felt in communities and neighborhoods throughout the country. The Jacksonville-based mortgage company helped more than 80,000 families with their home financing in 1993, and that number will continue to grow tremendously each year.

BancBoston has deep roots in the Jacksonville community, going back more than 100 years to the Telfair Stockton Company which handled much of the property on which Northeast Florida railroads were built. Telfair later became Stockton, Whatley, Davin & Co., a mortgage company that developed the historic and elegant Avondale and San Marco neighborhoods. BancBoston was formed in 1988 when four individual mortgage companies owned by Bank of Boston, including Stockton, Whatley, Davin & Co., were combined. BancBoston is a wholly-owned subsidiary of Bank of Boston.

Today, BancBoston Mortgage operates mortgage lending outlets in 27 national markets including Seattle, San Jose, Houston, Atlanta, Charlotte, Providence and Milwaukee as well as Jacksonville and seven additional Florida cities. More than 800 people work in the Jacksonville headquarters, and a majority of those people are given the responsibility of servicing the company's mortgage loans. To date, BancBoston is handling 330,000 loans that represent a portfolio of more than $23 billion. The company is an approved servicer for Fannie Mae, Freddie Mac, Ginnie Mae and private investors. BancBoston handles loans in 46 states and ranks in the top 20 in originating and servicing size in the United States.

The company is poised for even greater growth as it moves into the most exciting years in its history. While other financial institutions are struggling to break even, BancBoston has posted record earnings. The corporation is recognized as a forerunner in leading-edge technology for communications and computerized processing. Customers have access to their loan information 24 hours a day, seven days a week. And BancBoston has set the benchmark for streamlined processing in its backshop procedures and rapid loan approvals, offering homebuyers the option to close in as few as 15 days from the time of application. The company is continually finding new ways to make buying a home faster and easier with technology such as laptop computer applications and loan status tracking.

As a major employer in Jacksonville, BancBoston supports community organizations such as the United Way, Volunteer Jacksonville, the Jacksonville Symphony, the Urban League and Junior Achievement. When disaster strikes BancBoston customers, the company supports relief operations. When hurricanes struck South Florida and Charleston, BancBoston sent in teams to help ensure speedy processing of the victims hazard insurance, and supplies were sent to aid the communities. And when flooding saturated the Midwest, BancBoston employees volunteered to help.

The company also supports the next generation through a close partnership with students at Wolfson High School in Jacksonville. BancBoston employees serve on a school advisory board, students work at the company in summer internships and the students are invited to shadow employees for a day to get a stronger sense of the mortgage industry and the world of work.

BancBoston is committed to supporting the growth of Northeast Florida as the company's own growth continues across the country at an impressive pace.

BancBoston Mortgage Corporation

Over time, the winds of change have reshaped the hotel industry. A variety of new hotel options now dot the landscape. As Jacksonville's business community has grown, so, too, has the need for special accommodations for business travelers and consultants who may be staying weeks or months to complete transactions. Corporate travelers want high-tech office equipment at hand, and they also prefer a setting that is welcoming and home-like to make extended times on the road more pleasant.

Homewood Suites Hotel opened its doors in Jacksonville in 1991with an all-suite hotel on the Southside, the city's bustling suburban office center. Jacksonville's Homewood Suites Hotel is part of the Memphis-based Promus Corp., a hotel chain with all-suite hotels in 24 cities around the country.

The 116 suites in Jacksonville offer guests the chance to relax and unwind in a setting that's so close to home travelers can even smell the muffins baking in the oven.

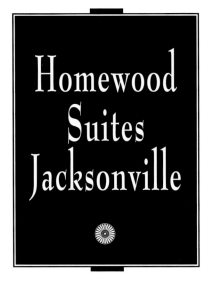

Homewood Suites Jacksonville

For business travelers who need to work "after hours," Homewood Suites has a 24-hour "Executive Center" that offers free use of a personal computer loaded with popular software, a full-sized conference table and typewriter and copier. The hotel is designed to make a business travelers stay as productive and enjoyable as possible.

At Homewood, the spacious suites are designed with completely separate bedrooms and full kitchens complete with home-size refrigerator and ice-maker, microwave, twin-burner range, toaster oven, coffeemaker and dishwasher. Fully-stocked cabinets include all the cookware, flatware, glasses and dishes guests need for a stay of just a few days, or an extended stay lasting weeks or months.

By locating on Jacksonville's growing Southside, Homewood Suites is in the heart of the cities "new downtown," the major suburban office-park area that is home to offices of nearly all the major companies in the area. It's also one of the city's most popular

Homewood Suites

suburban dining, shopping and cultural areas. The hotel is located on Baymeadows Road, just west of Interstate 95, at the entrance to Deerwood Center.

Northeast Florida has been a favorite for corporate relocations for the past decade. So, when families come to explore the neighborhoods and look for new homes, Jacksonville's Homewood Suites Hotel offers a setting where the whole family can stay in comfort. There are several types of suites with one or two bedrooms and enhanced one-bedroom floorplans with expanded kitchens and woodburning fireplaces.

Guests can start each morning with a compli-

mentary, continental breakfast buffet featuring our own freshly baked muffins and end the day with a bite to eat at our free hospitality hour, during which guests enjoy complimentary beverages (including beer and wine), as well as hors d'oeuvres and dinner items. Recreation is available in a fully-equipped exercise facilities and outdoor recreational amenities (full-size pool, spa and basketball/volleyball court).

Jacksonville's Homewood Suites Hotel combines the amenities of a superior hotel with the finishing touches of home at surprisingly affordable rates.

As the official hotel of The Players Club (TPC) at Sawgrass and the ATP Tour International Headquarters, the magnificent 4,800-acre Marriott at Sawgrass Resort creates a unique resort collection — the flavors of sophistication and super sports savored with a tropical savage twist.

Located just south of Jacksonville in plush Ponte Vedra Beach, the award-winning Marriott at Sawgrass Resort has recently been named the "Number One Golf Resort Value in America" by *Money* magazine and also boasts Successful Meetings Pinnacle Award, Meetings & Conventions Gold Key and Gold Tee Awards, AAA Four-Diamond and Mobil Four-Star rating.

Only a stroke away from the world's most renowned sports organizations, the Marriott at Sawgrass is the second largest golf resort in the United States with 99 incredible holes. Featuring five championship golf courses, lobby golf operations and pro shop, four driving ranges and six putting greens to choose from — including a unique 18-hole on-property executive green — the Marriott at Sawgrass offers the ultimate resort contrast for a golfer's getaway — a mix that is pleasurable for both the proficient golfer and weekend duffer.

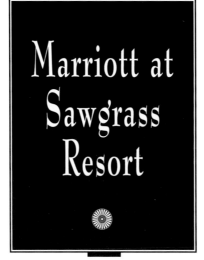

Marriott at Sawgrass Resort

For families, the Marriott at Sawgrass Resort is best known as "One of the Top 50 Family Resorts" by *Better Homes and Gardens* with tennis, beach fun, horseback riding, shopping and special programs for children and teenagers.

The resort offers 538 guest rooms, suites, golf and beachfront villas; five restaurants and lounges; and the largest meeting and convention facility between Atlanta and Orlando with an impressive 40,000 square feet. The resort's newest addition, the Island Green Pavilion is a 5,100 square-foot reception arena nearly encircled by water, decks and panoramic views, offering the perfect place to meet or entertain.

The Marriott at Sawgrass portrays its twist of "primitive posh" excitement in every resort aspect — activities, food, interiors, exteriors and atmosphere. The resort is bordered by two and one-half miles of pristine beach to the east and salt-water marshes and the Intracoastal Waterway to the west.

For unparalleled play with a blend of subtle sophistication, call (904) 285-7777 or (800) 457-GOLF.

Marriott at Sawgrass Resort

Sprint/United Telephone-Florida is guided by a simple, yet powerful vision: To be the company customers instinctively turn to for information and communications solutions.

In order to achieve that vision, Sprint/United Telephone opened its doors for business in Jacksonville in early 1993. By the end of that year, the size of the sales force in the market doubled and will continue to grow to meet the needs of its customers.

The entry of Sprint/United Telephone into the Jacksonville market heralded the beginning of a new era for the company and for the area. No longer were businesses in Northeast Florida limited when it came to choosing a telecommunications partner. As part of the Sprint family of companies, Sprint/United offered customers the choice of working with a company small enough to offer individualized service, while still being backed by a global telecommunications leader.

The distinction Sprint/United offers is its approach to customers. The company empha-

potential impact the company poses is staggering when considering the fact that Sprint/United is backed by Sprint, a $10.5 billion diversified international telecommunications leader.

Also, by opening the Jacksonville office, as well as offices in Tampa and Fort Lauderdale, Sprint/United Telephone completed its goal of covering the state as these new offices joined forces with existing offices serving central Florida, Fort Myers and Ocala.

In Jacksonville, Sprint/United Telephone is a major Cornerstone investor with the Chamber of Commerce and serves on the Economic Development Council. A participant in upgrading Florida's schools through the educational program Blueprint 2000, Sprint/United is helping bring integrated voice, data and video capabilities to the classroom.

Part of the company's commitment to the overall well-being of the area is an ever-increasing investment in the minority community. Sprint/United sponsors minority internships and offers bilingual customer service and telemarketing throughout the state.

Why take such an interest in the quality of life and economic well-being of Northeast Florida? It's simple. The people at Sprint/United Telephone understand that before customers "instinctively" turn to their company, their company has to prove itself as a respected corporate citizen and neighbor; and that's a goal they plan to obtain.

Sprint/United Tel.

sizes face-to-face individual consultations with customers to solve business communications problems and design integrated network systems that not only meet today's needs, but will serve as springboards for future solutions. For everything from voice to data to video communications, the company concentrates on exceptional service and the latest technology to develop the best possible system for each individual business.

With more than 6,000 employees, and nearly 1.5 million local telephone subscribers in 36 counties, Sprint/United's economic impact in Florida is considerable. Statewide, the company has invested more than $2.7 billion in plant and equipment. And the

Sprint/United Tel.

Swift advances in technology and dynamic business growth characterize Continental Cablevision's 10 years of service to Jacksonville. Homes with cable have more than doubled to over 200,000. A 4,800-mile network of coaxial and fiber optic cable continues to reach outward into every corner of the community. And the company's product line of video, audio and digital data services has expanded dramatically.

But in the end, the folks at Continental Cablevision of Jacksonville believe that it still comes down to people.

"We define success as an effective focus on customers and community," explains W. Scott Westerman, vice president and district manager of the Jacksonville operation. "The way we do it is to put the decision makers as close to the customer as possible."

Service is the heart of Continental Cablevision's corporate philosophy. It's reflected in the "Seal of Good Customer Service" awarded to the company by the National Cable Television Association and by a subscriber poll in *Cablevision* magazine that named Continental the nation's best run cable operator for three years in a row. But it begins with a rigorous training program that all employees complete during their first month on the job.

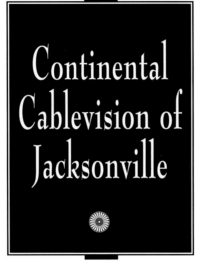

Continental Cablevision of Jacksonville

Hagy. "Our ongoing professional development program ensures that employees at all levels provide superior service to their customers."

According to Westerman, the term "customer" has a broad definition. "For the leadership team, customers are the people who are at the front lines. Our whole reason for being is to give them the support they need."

Volunteerism is another hallmark of Continental's service philosophy. According to Community Relations Director Dave Reid: "A high percentage of our workforce share their talents with the community. You'll find a Continental connection in just about every organization in town."

The major emphasis is on education. The company's "Cable in the Classroom" initiative began five years ago with a goal to provide free service to area schools. Since then, Continental has wired more than 200 school buildings in Duval and St. Johns counties, and has developed a mechanism to disseminate information on 500 hours of educational programming to teachers each month. Jane Fleetwood, Continental's community education coordinator says the commitment doesn't stop there. "We fund a number of educational initiatives including an awards program for innovative use of television in the

Cable in the Classroom.

Continental Cablevision

"We focus on developing interpersonal and problem-solving skills that provide each of our 530 associates the confidence to do what they think is right," says Human Resources and Training Director Susan

classroom, 10 college scholarships for local high school students, and an internship program that provides employment for college-bound minorities who are planning a career in business."

Programming

Another community connection is centered in the company's local programming department. One hundred seventy-three broadcast hours are produced each week on Continental's public access and local origination channels. Most focus on local issues from senior citizens news to firefighter training, but several programs have had international viewership. Continental employees helped a group of fourth and fifth graders at Loretto Elementary produce a documentary on life in Jacksonville. The show was broadcast on Russian television and won a national *Reader's Digest* award.

Boston-based Continental Cablevision Inc. is the nation's largest privately-held cable communications firm. Continental Cablevision of Jacksonville Inc. was created in 1984 with the purchase of Area Communications Inc., Jacksonville's first cable company. Area began cable service in 1979.

In the beginning, cable television's primary benefit was improved reception of broadcast television signals. Today, Jacksonville subscribers can choose from more than 50 different channels, including cable originals like CNN, The Weather Channel, ESPN and C-

SPAN. Special premium video services are also available including HBO, Cinemax, Showtime, The Disney Channel, and pay-per-view services that allow viewers to order individual movies and special events from the comfort of their living rooms.

The newest cable product available in Jacksonville is Digital Cable Radio. DCR subscribers receive more than 30 channels of commercial free digital quality audio. Music formats include classical favorites, pop, solid gold, jazz, show tunes, Latin and reggae. The service also provides international spoken word programming from the BBC World Service plus digital simulcasts of HBO, Cinemax, Showtime, MTV and VH-1.

"The rapid growth in multi-channel communications technology means that today's consumer has more choice, and higher expectations than ever before," Westerman says. "One thing that hasn't changed over the years is our objective of surpassing customer expectations. Continental people make that happen. It's the secret of our past success and the key to our future."

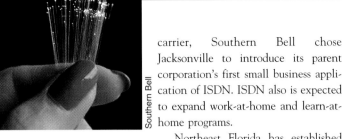

Southern Bell is in the midst of a $200 million upgrade of its telecommunications network in Northeast Florida, a vital advance in the economic environment of Florida's First Coast.

To understand the scope of the investment, just consider that Jacksonville's 24,000 miles of fiber optic lines were expanded by 7,500 in 1993 alone.

These expenditures will have a direct impact on the economy of the region. This impact is twofold. First, it puts service reliability at levels not even imagined 10 years ago. Second, Southern Bell's network will meet its customers' exploding requirements for bandwidth, a measurement of lightwave data transmissions, and new services. This combination creates a healthier environment for existing business and for attracting new business to the First Coast.

State-of-the-art telecommunications technology in the First Coast is a key element in economic development. "One reason Jacksonville is so attractive to so many large corporations that are relocating is often overlooked — the technology," says University of North Florida President Adam Herbert, immediate past chairman of the Jacksonville Chamber of Commerce.

For existing businesses, the enhanced technology will mean the ability to upgrade services. The architecture of Integrated Switched Digital Networks, ISDN, allows enormous labor-saving applications: workstation/telephone integration, high-speed file transfer, remote local access network (LAN), multiscreen sharing, voice annotated document transfer, and video conferencing.

Small businesses benefit, too. As a local exchange carrier, Southern Bell chose Jacksonville to introduce its parent corporation's first small business application of ISDN. ISDN also is expected to expand work-at-home and learn-at-home programs.

Northeast Florida has established itself as a regional healthcare cluster and Southern Bell's technology is serving the medical industry. Teleradiology is a likely medical application allowing two physicians in separate locations to examine the same X-ray simultaneously.

Recently, Southern Bell's parent company, BellSouth teamed with the developers of the Jacksonville International Tradeport on the Northside to plan state-of-the-art infrastructure for the business park. Called FirstPark Services[sm], it provides access to high-speed digital data switching, fiber optic transmission, imaging technology and a broad array of capabilities from voice mail to video-conferencing.

All this new technology brings another important advantage to the table: reliability.

Optical fiber cable is immune to electromagnetic interference and most water damage, thereby minimizing service problems and reducing errors in voice and data transmissions. When Hurricane Andrew devastated South Florida, Southern Bell was able to restore service rapidly and continue to maintain an operational network.

Southern Bell, with its 3,300 employees in Northeast Florida, has been a leading corporate citizen in the region since 1880. Southern Bell is aggressively doing everything it can to strengthen its telecommunications network so Florida's First Coast can compete globally for new jobs and businesses of the 21st century.

It's uncommon to find a woman in the driver's seat of a big rig and even more unusual to find a female at the helm of a trucking company. But after piloting trucks herself for three years, Audrey Quackenbush became the driving force behind White Line Trucking Inc., a specialized carrier headquartered in Jacksonville.

Northeast Florida has proven to be a great location for the 10-year-old trucking firm. Poised at the northern edge of Florida, Jacksonville is a gateway for a great deal of trucking traffic on its way down into the state and upward throughout the southeast and west. The area's active industrial base and major port provides plenty of customers as do the three Navy bases in the city. In 1993, White Line Trucking brought in nearly $2 million in revenues, and Quackenbush hopes to double the size of the operations over the next five years.

Quackenbush started driving commercial loads around the country in 1979. After three years, she worked for a number of trucking lines, dispatching vehicles, devising schedules, overseeing purchasing and generally running the offices. Ambitious and encouraged by key clients to start her own business, in 1983 she established a trucking agency where she served as a middleman, lining up customers with a number of trucking lines. Then, in 1990 White Line became a full-fledge trucking company, which now has four office employees and 25 truckers,

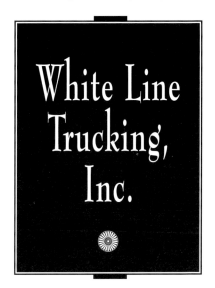

half of whom operate as independent contractors.

The company hauls every thing from wire cable to jet engines to construction equipment. About 68 percent of its freight is tied to the military, which has come to rely on White Line Trucking to deliver jet engines and squadron parts. The company is also known for its specialized emergency on-time deliveries. Clients can contact Quackenbush 24-hours a day if necessary for quick transfer of a product. For example, a power plant may need a piece of equipment to quickly repair its machinery within a few hours or otherwise face a costly plant shutdown. Freight is transferred to 48 states, but a bulk of the traffic moves within the Southeastern states, north to Virginia and west to Texas.

While Quackenbush receives plenty of attention because she's a woman in a male-dominated industry, she's refreshingly relaxed about the gender issues. But she has become acutely sensitive to the difficulties facing small businesses. Her interest in the concerns of small firms led to her 1993 appointment to Jacksonville Chamber of Commerce's Small Business Department board.

While heading the company, she remains in touch with the every-day aspects of the operations. It's not unusual to find Quackenbush dispatching trucks, and she maintains her Commercial Driver's License. At times, the CEO has had to take to the road. She explains, "When it comes down to it, I drive."

Below the streets of Jacksonville lie hundreds of miles of gas mains that supply much of the energy needs of Jacksonville's major manufacturers and thousands of city residents.

Peoples Gas System is the city's natural gas supplier, serving 17,250 customers — 14,000 of whom are residences. The firm is also a major supplier of propane gas in areas not served by natural gas mains. By far, the bulk of Peoples' gas supply in Jacksonville (more than 95 percent) is distributed to businesses, particularly to large industrial manufacturers.

The company has seen unprecedented growth in recent years in its commercial business because of the economy of gas compared with other fuels. Today, Peoples serves nearly every major manufacturer and hospital in the greater Jacksonville area, and continues to expand to meet the needs of new commercial customers.

One of Peoples' largest customers in Jacksonville is the Jacksonville Electric Authority, which uses natural gas to fuel its massive generators. The electric authority uses approximately 15 percent of Peoples' total annual gas distribution in Jacksonville.

Baptist Medical Center in Jacksonville uses natural gas for its in-house cogeneration plant which supplies their electricity and thermal power needs. This two-million-square-foot facility is the world's largest cogeneration hospital.

In one of its most significant expansions ever, Peoples recently completed construction of 23 miles of high-pressure main to serve the JEA and other major northside customers such as U.S. Gypsum and Anheuser-Busch. This was in addition to 6.3 miles of 24 inch gas main installed on Hecksher Drive to serve the JEA Northside plant. The pipeline is the largest-diameter main installed in Florida since 1959. The project also involved underwater crossings of the Trout River and two additional creeks.

Peoples Gas in Jacksonville is part of the statewide Peoples Gas System Inc., headquartered in Tampa. The firm, with 11 offices, is the largest natural gas distributor in Florida, totalling more than $200 million in sales revenue annually. Its affiliate, Peoples Gas Company, is also the state's largest independent propane distributor. Peoples has a statewide employment of more than 1,100.

Previously serving primarily South Florida and the Gulf Coast of Florida, Peoples expanded into northeast Florida in 1979 with the purchase of Florida Gas Company. Florida Gas had a long histo-

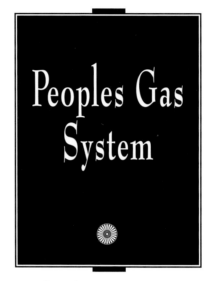

Peoples Gas System

ry of supplying Jacksonville with its natural gas needs.

The gas industry in Jacksonville dates back to 1854, the year the Citizens Gaslight Company began manufacturing gas from coal and pumping it through hollowed-out cypress logs to light the streets of the city. The enterprise later became known as the Jacksonville Gas Corporation. In 1958 a natural gas pipeline was constructed to Jacksonville and the firm was purchased and renamed Florida Gas Company.

The Jacksonville division receives gas to serve the city through four gate stations, including the city gate in the Normandy section of the city's west side. At the gate stations, gas is measured and regulated into the Jacksonville system from the statewide transmission pipelines. Transmission companies pipe the natural gas in from the rich gas fields of Texas, Louisiana, and the Gulf of Mexico.

In Jacksonville, Peoples employs nearly 100 people in its four major departments:

The Distribution Department is responsible for laying the underground pipes to extend gas service around the city to a growing number of commercial customers.

The Service Department serves primarily residential customers. Through the department, service lines and house piping are connected to the main lines; gas appliances are installed and repaired; and residential gas systems are adjusted and serviced.

The Sales Department offers a full line of gas appliances — including ranges, water heaters, clothes dryers, furnaces, central heat and air conditioning, and others.

Large industrial accounts are served primarily by the Administrative Department, as are other essential financial and personnel concerns of the operation.

In the future, Peoples Gas System, both locally and statewide, will continue to expand its facilities and strengthen its service and distribution capabilities to meet the increasing demand for gas as an energy source.

Peoples Gas has obtained approval from the Florida Public Service Commission for a Natural Gas Vehicle Program. Federal and state legislation mandates alternative fuel vehicle usage, citing both the Energy Policy and Clean Air Acts. The Company is a part of a statewide move to build an infrastructure of facilities that will support the increased demand for these clean-burning fuels.

Peoples Gas is also implementing a statewide program utilizing natural gas for an energy source in gas-fired chillers and air-conditioning equipment. This program will reduce energy costs and help to conserve our environment by utilizing user-friendly refrigerants.

Both of these programs insure that Peoples Gas is continually looking for ways to conserve our environment, reduce energy costs and become less dependent on foreign fuels.

At age 25, a bright and ambitious Barbara Samson was working as a salesperson for a Florida long-distance company. Working with large corporate clients, she saw that companies wanted alternatives. Samson envisioned a niche in telecommunications: Providing businesses with a competitive alternative to local telephone companies by offering businesses a direct connection to their long distance carrier(s) and to their other business locations.

Samson started Tampa-based Intermedia Communications of Florida Inc. in 1987 and now the company is the leading provider of competitive access services in Florida. Intermedia operates in five major Florida business cities. The company started with Orlando in 1988, then added Tampa in 1989, Miami in 1990, Jacksonville in 1992 and St. Petersburg in 1993. In 1992, Intermedia went public, offering shares on the NASDAQ, and has raised more than $40 million for further growth.

Communications systems clearly have become one of the most highly competitive markets in the modern economy. Intermedia has not hesitated in challenging restrictions on competition or facing off with the baby Bells. The company hopes that continued easing of restrictions by federal regulators will

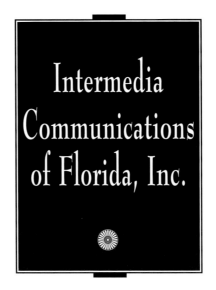

Barbara Samson, Senior Vice President

soon allow for even more expansion of its services.

Intermedia picked Jacksonville as the setting for its fourth metropolitan fiber optic network in 1992 by leasing conduit and pole space from the Jacksonville Electric Authority. The company then began linking businesses such as the Florida East Coast Railroad and BancBoston Mortgage Corp. to long-distance carriers and to their other business locations. More than 70 miles of fiber optic cable have been deployed in Jacksonville, creating rings that provide security against network outages. Intermedia currently connects to more than 40 buildings in the city and is planning to add many more.

Intermedia selected Jacksonville because of its growing business environment and large concentration of major corporate headquarters and regional offices. Among the Jacksonville customers: The Federal Reserve Bank, Merrill Lynch, The Prudential, the City of Jacksonville and Cellular One to name a few. A state-of-the-art network also links Jacksonville to the other Florida cities where Intermedia has established fiber optic systems.

Intermedia offers businesses a wide variety of competitively priced telecommunication services — from increased reliability and protection from network outages to higher quality, greater flexibility

BancBoston Mortgage Building

and improved integrity of voice, data and video transmission.

Florida Trend business magazine in 1992 said: "Intermedia...is at the forefront of what, inevitably, will be the future in telecommunications. And, to a large extent, Intermedia's business is at the center of what may determine whether Florida is a leading state in attracting new business and becoming a competitive player in the Information Age."

Federal Building

USA Today business columnist Dan Dorfman told readers in August 1993 that Intermedia was a company to watch for impressive gains through 1994.

Samson, now senior vice president, said: "We've built an asset here in five cities in Florida, we've tied them all together with an enhanced network, and now we're assessing going outside of the state of Florida. The opportunities for growth and bringing on new services is unbelievable. We have the people in place, we have access to capital and we are just going to grow and grow and grow this business in whatever way makes the most sense."

Independent Life Building

Barnett Center

As you drive through the various quaint and charming neighborhoods that rest on both sides of the imposing St. Johns River, you cannot help but see the distinctive red, white and blue 'For Sale' and 'Sold' signs that blanket the Jacksonville real estate market.

These signs have become the symbol of success, not only for individual home owners and home buyers, but also for one of the city's most successful corporations.

Established in 1965, Watson Realty Corporation, the largest independently-owned real estate brokerage firm in North Florida, has seen its total sales volume hit the $7.5 billion mark at the beginning of the 1990s.

Starting as a one-man operation, William A. Watson, Jr. put together a winning formula of commitment to customer service and the determination to succeed, that has resulted in the establishment of more than 40 sales and administrative offices, stretching from St. Marys, Georgia, and going all the way to Orlando, Florida. As a result, the company has been ranked as the largest real estate firm in Jacksonville, in the top five in the state, and in the top 30 in the nation.

According to Bill Watson, just putting up a 'For Sale' sign is no longer enough. Under his leadership, the company has been on the leading edge of sales and service innovation through what is known as The Watson Way.

Choosing a new home versus an existing home, determining the appropriate financing, conducting market analysis, coordinating the closing process... these are the services addressed by a highly-trained and knowledgeable Watson sales team.

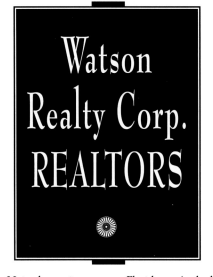

This team is armed with an arsenal of innovative sales tools that include specialized company publications highlighting properties; a dominance in broadcast and classified newspaper advertising; weekly property exposure on cable television's Real Estate Channel; the company's Bridge Loan program that assists buyers with their financing; and, the Watson Real Estate Hotline that gives buyers 24 hour access through their phones on selling features of Watson homes, just to name a few.

As a full-service real estate firm, Watson Realty has put together a strong Relocation Division. For the corporate client who needs to coordinate the move of many employees or for individuals, Watson Realty can take care of every phase of the relocation process. As part of the Homequity Relocation Network, the nation's largest referral service, Watson Realty can handle relocation services all over the country.

Watson Realty's Commercial Division serves the business and real estate investment needs of individuals and companies looking to invest in North and Central Florida. And the Property Management Division serves the needs of various company and individual owners through services ranging from rent collection to property maintenance.

Watson Realty takes pride in being the number one lister and seller of homes in Jacksonville. Through The Watson Way, it is the company's goal to provide every current and prospective client with the best possible services and attention when it comes to their real estate needs.

Watson 'Sold' signs are a familiar sight in Jacksonville neighborhoods, especially with 24 hour selling through the Watson Real Estate Hotline information service.

Watson Realty Corporation, which consists of three operating regions — Jacksonville, North Central Florida and Central Florida, is headquartered at 11226-1 San Jose Boulevard.

Special magazines published by Watson Realty are just one of many innovative sales techniques used by the company to market Jacksonville homes.

Watson Realty was founded by William A. Watson, Jr. (left). The Relocation Division is headed by Michael Taylor (right).

As one of the oldest Southeast firms specializing in commercial real estate, CARTER is one of the most active and productive real estate firms in the region. The Atlanta-based company's total volume of sales, leasing, and build-to-suit developments consistently place CARTER among the top five real estate firms in the Southeast.

CARTER opened its Jacksonville office in 1990. Among other clients, CARTER is the leasing agent for the Barnett Tower, the tallest building in Jacksonville's downtown skyline. The firm also leases and manages a number of office parks, a distribution complex and has distinctive properties for sale. Representative clients include Bell South, First Union National Bank of Florida, Computer Power Inc. and Equitable Life Insurance Company. CARTER has offices in Charlotte, Nashville and Birmingham in addition to the Jacksonville office and its Atlanta headquarters.

Since its founding in 1958 by Frank Carter, the company has developed significant capabilities and a solid track record in meeting the needs of varied clients. Carter offers the following services: Counseling, Management, Investment, Leasing, Development, and Brokerage.

The company is owned and operated by its six top executives and employs about 615 people. Through an ownership position in ONCOR International, a real estate network, CARTER provides services in markets throughout the United States, Canada and western Europe.

CARTER's record and reputation reflect the training, capability, and commitment of its people to perform in the best interests of its clients. In 1992, the company transacted more than 7 million square feet in leases totaling more than $334 million in volume and represented investors in acquisitions and dispositions of properties totaling more than $131 million in volume. Recognizing the value of its client relationships, CARTER has assembled a management portfolio totaling 17 million square feet of office, industrial, and retail space and has developed in excess of $2 billion in real estate in 17 cities throughout the Southeast.

While striving to provide economic rewards for its clients, CARTER also seeks to enhance the quality of life in communities like Jacksonville which it serves.

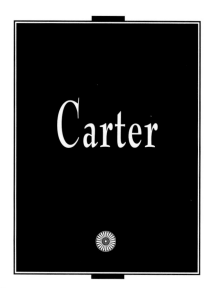

Carter

Carter

Carter

University Medical Center (UMC), a 528-bed, major teaching hospital serving Northeast Florida and Southeast Georgia, has been fulfilling the health care needs of Jacksonville and the surrounding communities since 1870. In 1988 the hospital was designated the Urban Campus for the University of Florida Health Science Center. Today, 14 medical residency programs are offered to more than 250 resident physicians who are receiving advanced training in their areas of specialty.

As an innovator in health care, UMC provides state-of-the-art services unequaled in Northeast Florida. These services include a Level I trauma center and Level III neonatal intensive care unit (NICU), each the highest level. Both the trauma and neonatal programs benefit from a helicopter-air ambulance service — TraumaOne — based at UMC. A trauma team, including doctors, nurses, paramedics and support personnel, is stationed in the hospital 24 hours a day, 365 days a year as well. Other areas of emphasis include cardiovascular and peripheral vascular services, the neurosciences, women's and children's services and cancer services.

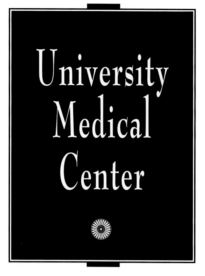

A prenatal diagnostic program is provided to women with pregnancy-related problems, including histories of family birth defects and advanced maternal age. Also available is genetic counseling, making possible the early detection of chromosomal and structural defects in the unborn child.

The Florida Poison Information Center/Jacksonville is located on the UMC campus. By Florida statute there are three poison centers in the state, each at Level I trauma centers. Jacksonville's center at UMC provides 24-hour access to emergency poisoning information in addition to conducting poison prevention education programs throughout the 904 area code. This staff includes specially-trained nurses, pharmacists and board-certified toxicologists.

Because UMC is a major affiliate of the University of Florida Health Science Center, the attending physician staff is composed of University of Florida faculty physicians. In addition to overseeing the graduate medical education programs, these physicians also participate in research and the clinical practice of medicine. Some of this clinical practice takes place in the University of Florida Faculty Clinic located on the campus of UMC. Many subspecialty services not found elsewhere in Northeast Florida are located in the Faculty Clinic.

The mission of University Medical Center is to provide excellent, high-quality health care in the most cost-effective manner and to provide an environment

Univ. Med. Center

Univ. Med. Center

for the teaching of medical personnel and other health professionals. UMC participates in many managed care contracts in order to maintain a competitive stature.

UMC also provides primary care and treatment in 97 subspecialty services. The resident physicians working in these clinics further their education under the supervision of approximately 190 full-time faculty physicians and more than 190 community-based physicians.

UMC, as the University of Florida Urban Campus, has adopted the following values as part of the Continuous Quality Improvement process: Honesty, Respect, Teamwork, Compassion, Creativity,

Communication, Responsibility, Competency, Trust and Excellence. Each and every employee is brought on board knowing the definition of each of these and their importance to total quality.

UMC's customers, whether internal or external, are of paramount importance and are the focal point of all health care activities. University Medical Center and its employees are poised to meet the 21st century with the very best in quality health care. The University of Florida and its colleges of Medicine, Nursing, Dentistry and Pharmacy are our partners in this commitment for the future.

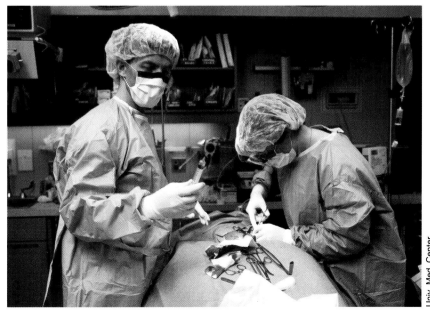

Univ. Med. Center

In the last quarter-century, Jacksonville has emerged as one of the most dynamic medical communities in the Southeast. Among the area's most prominent health care providers, the Memorial health care system has proven to be a vital contributor, providing comprehensive medical services to a growing population and rapidly changing marketplace. To accomplish its goals, a synergistic network of hospitals, clinics and support facilities operates under the strategic direction of Memorial's parent company, Health South Inc.

Memorial was founded in 1969 by four business executives and four physicians led by Dr. J. Brooks Brown. From its inception, Memorial has developed innovative ways to blend human compassion with the latest medical technology. Today, as CEO of Health South, Dr. Brown shuns "status quo" thinking to focus on the future of quality medical care on Florida's First Coast.

"An important part of our corporate vision is to provide leadership in working with others to improve the health of our community," says Dr. Brown. "We see Continuous Quality Improvement (CQI) as a business strategy that's vital to long-term success. By sharing knowledge and expertise, we believe it's possible to raise our community's quality of life to meet almost every expectation."

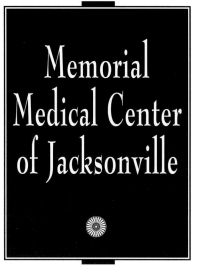

Memorial Medical Center of Jacksonville

Located near the intersection of Beach and University boulevards, Memorial Medical Center of Jacksonville (MMCJ) is a 353-bed, not-for-profit hospital providing a wide range of medical and surgical services such as oncology, cardiology, women's services, orthopedics, critical care, and level II emergency service. President Charles E. Evans' leadership has made CQI an integral part of Memorial's corporate culture. "Change is inevitable, but by understanding our customers' needs for both today and tomorrow, we can continuously improve our products and services to exceed their expectations," said Evans.

Memorial Outpatient Services: the diagnostic and imaging team employs the most advanced methods for

Memorial's commitment to continuous quality improvement is a team effort involving every employee, physician and administrator to improve our community's quality of life. (Memorial Medical)

accurate and dependable diagnosis. The hospital's sophisticated medical imaging capabilities include MRI, CTscan, PETscan, SPECT, nuclear medicine and radiology.

When treatment and surgical procedures can be accomplished without an overnight hospital stay, MMCJ's outpatient center provides an economical and convenient alternative. The service accommodates every surgical specialty in a setting that is patient-friendly and comfortable.

Memorial Women's Services: providing an array of family health services tailored specifically for women has been a hallmark of MMCJ. The birth rooms combine a relaxing, home-like setting with the most sophisticated medical technology available. The sophisticated assisted-fertility program, the first in our region, has helped more than 100 couples conceive.

Since patient education plays a key role in health care, Women's Services offers a full complement of classes at the MMCJ main campus and throughout the community. Topics range from childbirth and sibling preparation to breast self-examination, nutrition and support groups.

Memorial Oncology Services: stressing cancer survival through aggressive treatment and ongoing education is the daily mission of this dedicated team. With its specialized outpatient services, pharmacy and tumor registry, MMCJ teams battle all types of cancer through chemotherapy, radiotherapy and surgery. Patients can also participate in a variety of clinical trials that test promising new cancer-fighting drugs and treatments.

Memorial Cardiovascular Services: prevention and treatment of heart disease receive special attention at MMCJ, where the Critical Care and Open-heart Recovery units rank as two of the most advanced and efficient in the First Coast. MMCJ was one of 30 U.S. hospitals chosen to participate in clinical trials of a new generation of clot-dissolving drugs which could increase heart attack survival rates. The Memorial Chest Pain Service, located in the emergency department, provides fast, efficient care for patients who arrive at the emergency room suf-

Located at the intersection of Beach and University boulevards, Memorial Medical Center is recognized for its outstanding health care in a wide variety of specialized services.

fering from chest pain.

The "Paperless" Hospital: an advanced electronic information and communication system links physicians, staff and administrators of each facility in our health care network. It provides medical staff and outcomes data to improve efficiency of patient care, in addition to easily accessible and retrievable electronic medical records.

American International Health Alliance: joining with other First Coast health care providers, MMCJ provides equipment, supplies and professional support to three hospitals in Murmansk, Russia. The unique partnership provides a valuable learning opportunity and extends the First Coast's healthy medical climate north of the Arctic Circle.

Memorial Regional Rehabilitation Center

Since 1982, Memorial Regional Rehabilitation Center (MRRC) has built a reputation as our region's premier facility for recovery from traumatic injury or catastrophic illness. The center provides a full array of rehabilitation services for children and adults recovering from accidents, head and spinal cord injuries, stroke, amputation, neurological and orthopedic disorders and chronic pain.

Care teams of doctors, nurses, therapists and support staff work toward a single goal: to help each patient achieve an independent lifestyle. Every conceivable form of physical, emotional and psychological therapy is employed. A full-time teacher from the Duval County School System helps recovering children keep up with

Memorial's extensive array of advanced diagnostic technology serves thousands of First Coast patients every month of the year.

Since 1986, Memorial has led the development of outpatient care and surgery centers. Today, we serve the First Coast through facilities located in San Pablo, Regency and Mandarin communities.

schoolwork. Biofeedback services help patients exert control over stress and chronic pain — or teach new ways for muscles to function again.

MRRC opens a spectacular new rehabilitation hospital in 1994, on the north side of Memorial's University Boulevard campus. It will provide expanded, more efficient treatment programs for decades to come in an environment that is technologically superior and staffed by caring professionals.

Specialty Hospital of Jacksonville

As its name implies, Specialty Hospital of Jacksonville (SHJ) provides specialized care for patients who need long-term recovery in a hospital setting. Acquired in 1992, SHJ provides a unique and cost-effective approach to long-term acute care. While most SHJ patients are seriously ill, they are stable and no longer require the expensive critical care resources typically found in full-service hospitals and intensive care units.

Centrally located near Interstate 95 and University Boulevard,

The rehabilitation of injured people may be the most challenging mission in all of medicine. Memorial Regional Rehabilitation Center has built a reputation for results with both adult and pediatric patients. (Memorial Medical)

SHJ is geared for patients who are dependent on ventilators and other life support systems; those requiring long-term intravenous therapies; continuous nutritional support; serious skin conditions; and those with complex medical conditions. The facility accepts direct admissions and transfers patients whose recovery is expected to last 20 to 60 days or longer.

Patients receive highly personalized attention in a caring and informal environment. A variety of specialized therapies helps recovering patients progress toward independent functioning. Family members are encouraged to participate actively in this healing process.

Community Health Network

Memorial Health-Care Center at San Pablo represents an innovative concept that merges convenient, cost-effective health care with retail establishments, restaurants and even a supermarket. Opened in 1993, this new center exemplifies a Health South strategic policy to being efficient, high-quality medical services to local communities.

Located near the Intracoastal Waterway at Beach Boulevard and San Pablo Road, the facility serves as a focal point of a 26-acre shopping center called the Medical and Merchants Center. The first phase houses a central registration area, physicians' offices, physical rehabilitation, diagnostic and lab services, a pharmacy and community education area. Phase two will include outpatient surgery capabilities as well as sophisticated scanning equipment. A similar facility is under development in the Mandarin area.

Whenever you may need assistance, there's usually a member of the Memorial Auxiliary nearby to help. Their volunteer staffing and fund raising activities are vital to the health of our institution. **(Memorial Medical)**

Memorial HealthCare Park at Regency provides a convenient, outpatient medical imaging and physicians' offices facility where patients can receive a variety of diagnostic services, including radiology, MRI and CT scans. Located near Regency Square and the Dames Point Bridge, it makes Memorial's services more convenient to consumers and physicians in the Arlington and northside areas.

Memorial Health-Care Plaza, just south of the main campus, houses doctors' offices, diagnostic and treatment services for a variety of needs. The centerpiece is Memorial's Rehabilitation Outpatient Center for comprehensive adult and pediatric programs, including orthopedic rehabilitation; physical, occupational and speech therapy; neuro-psychological services; acute and chronic pain management; vocational services and physical medicine. At the Heart Fitness Center, specialists in exercise physiology help people develop wellness regiments tailored to their individual needs.

Memorial Health, Education and Research Foundation

A key component of our system is developing community support for enhancing services in the areas of patient care, advanced technology, health education and research. Nothing demonstrates the foundation's leadership more than The Time to Rebuild Lives capital campaign, which is raising funds for a new, multi-million-dollar rehabilitation center. The First Coast is fortunate to have such commitment and cooperation from employees, physicians, volunteers, board members and community leaders.

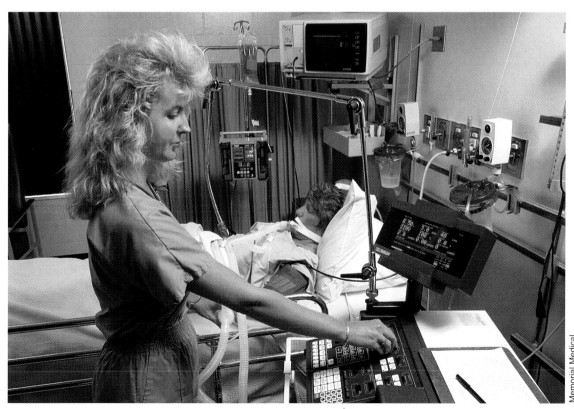

The first hospital of its kind in northeast Florida, Specialty Hospital of Jacksonville provides long-term hospital care for medically complex patients.

They weren't doctors or nurses. Yet in 1873, three Jacksonville women furnished a small cottage with beds, tables and chairs, and made a solemn vow: "To make this institution a place of refuge for the sick from all parts of the country." In this unlikely setting, they founded St. Luke's — Florida's first private hospital.

In the years that followed, the women raised money for a large building on Palmetto Street. They hired Florida's first female physician and established the state's first nursing school.

Throughout the next century, St. Luke's expanded to meet the needs of a growing community. The hospital moved from Palmetto to Eighth Street downtown, and in 1984 to Belfort Road on the city's growing southside. From humble beginnings, St. Luke's established a tradition of excellent healthcare in Jacksonville.

In 1987, Mayo Foundation chose St. Luke's as an affiliate and admitting hospital for Mayo Clinic Jacksonville. Today, on a 50-acre campus, two professional office buildings, the Mayo Family Medicine Center and a 24-hour Emergency Center complement the 289-bed hospital. The non-denominational hospital specializes in adult care procedures ranging from same-day surgeries to treatments like Bone Marrow Transplants requiring long-term hospitalizations.

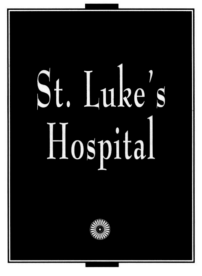

More than 600 physicians are on the medical staff. They include primary care physicians, specialists and surgeons from many medical practices throughout Jacksonville and Mayo Clinic Jacksonville.

The all-RN nursing staff is trained in many specialties, including oncology, cardiac and surgical intensive care. RNs are teamed with Patient Care Technicians, an innovative system which allows nurses to focus on critical medical needs. It's increased care without increased cost.

The hospital gives great consideration to patient environment. Every room is private. Service cabinets outside each room give nurses immediate access to supplies and charts without disturbing patients.

St. Luke's

Several units are designed to meet special needs. Since patients on the Bone Marrow Transplant Unit stay an average of three to four weeks, each room is equipped with a VCR, radio and exercise bike. The Epilepsy Monitoring Unit has soft surfaces to reduce the risk of injury to patients prone to seizures.

St. Luke's is recognized for advanced orthopedic, cardiovascular and reconstructive surgery. Three special orthopedic operating rooms have laminar air flow systems that constantly purify the air to reduce the risk of infection. The hospital is one of the few in the nation to provide stereotactic neurosurgery. This procedure uses a computer to help surgeons find and remove otherwise inoperable tumors deep within the brain.

Through the Ambulatory Care Unit, an outpatient can receive a wide variety of medical and surgical procedures such as hand, urological and eye surgery. Outpatients are pre-registered by RNs who explain procedures and respond to questions. These one-on-one consultations help patients feel at ease with their scheduled procedure.

St. Luke's is also known for high-tech diagnostics. One example is Functional Perfusion Imaging (FPI). St. Luke's is the only hospital in the Southeast to offer this non-invasive procedure which allows cardiologists to more accurately diagnose heart disease with simultaneous images of the heart's pump function and blood flow.

Education is playing an increasingly important role at St. Luke's. Medical, surgical and laboratory residents come from Mayo Graduate School of Medicine and other medical colleges nationwide to rotate through the hospital. St. Luke's is a member of the Council of Teaching Hospitals of the American Association of Medical Colleges.

With all that medical technology can offer, it remains the people who make the difference. And at St. Luke's the staff is dedicated to providing quality healthcare. With employees numbering more than 1,300, St. Luke's is listed as one of the area's largest employers. In addition to its staff, St. Luke's is fortunate to have an active Auxiliary. Founded in 1952, this group of women and men provide valuable service in more than 25 hospital areas.

And St. Luke's commitment to Jacksonville goes beyond patient care. The monthly Community Health Series invites the public to free programs on current health issues. A Speaker's Bureau takes programs out to groups and clubs. The hospital also co-sponsors the Avenue Striders, a mall-walking program, and throughout the year offers a variety of health screenings.

Today, the "refuge for the sick from all parts of the country" has exceeded its founders' goal. In addition to those from the local community, patients now come from many parts of the country and the world. Each one is welcomed with compassion, comfort, hope and healing.

In 1955, a new community hospital called Baptist Memorial Hospital was founded along the banks of the St. Johns River. The hospital has now grown into an integrated health system serving an entire region with three hospitals - Baptist Medical Center and the new Wolfson Children's Hospital on a centrally located, downtown riverfront and outpatient campus, and Baptist Medical Center - *Beaches*, which serves the growing Beaches area. In addition to this triad of complexes, the Baptist Doctor's Office Network brings primary medical care — family practice, pediatrics and internal medicine — to more than 21 neighborhoods throughout the greater Jacksonville area.

Since its modest beginnings, Baptist has developed specialized areas of care within its healthcare system, driven by physicians who represent almost every medical specialty. Primary specialty areas include oncology, cardiology, women's services, adult and pediatric emergency services, orthopaedics, ophthalmology, and pediatrics, to name just a few.

Baptist was the first hospital in the region to bring together a comprehensive cancer program, offering traditional and new modalities of cancer detection and treatment. Millions of dollars have been committed to the fight against cancer and the creation of state-of-the-art approaches to treatment of the disease through medical, radiation and surgical oncology. The Baptist Regional Cancer Institute offers advanced, research-based care plus a full range of diagnostic and support services in a central outpatient location. The Cancer Institute's research division is a leader in a number of projects sponsored by national cancer research organizations, including the National Cancer Institute, The Eastern Cooperative Oncology Group, the National Surgical Adjuvant Breast and Bowel Project, and the pharmaceutical industry. The Institute has designed and participated in many nationally recognized model programs, especially for breast, prostate, lung and brain cancers.

The Harden Cardiovascular Center provides full-service cardiology care and linkage of its services into participating hospitals throughout North

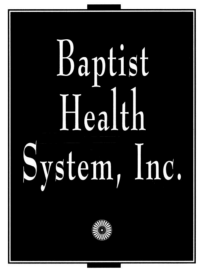

Baptist
Health
System, Inc.

Florida and South Georgia with the Heart Emergency Network. The network is a coordinated effort which provides immediate care for heart attack patients to lessen the chance of damage to the heart muscle, thus stabilizing them for further treatment at a major tertiary care center like Baptist, if needed. The National Heart Attack Risk Study, sponsored in the region by Baptist Medical Center, has encouraged additional community heart-health awareness by enrolling more than 15,000 people and screening them for their risk of heart disease.

Women's varied health needs are met at the Baptist Women's Pavilion, where a team of dedicated physicians, nurses and other medical professionals provide ultra-modern gynecological and obstetrical care. Each year, nearly 4,000 babies are born in The Wolfson Center for Mothers and Infants, which offers private delivery suites and comfortable birthing rooms with unparalleled maternity care. The Women's Resource Library is a community resource where major community programs on women's and family health issues, as well as a variety of support groups, are based; in addition, books, journals, videos and pamphlets on issues concerning women are available to the public at no charge.

Baptist has one of the busiest emergency centers in the South, and it offers an adult as well as a dedicated

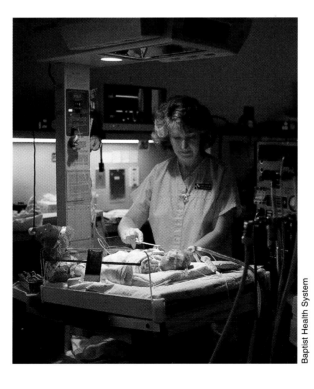

Children's Emergency Center, along with Jacksonville's only Hyperbaric Oxygen Chamber. Completing Baptist's emergency services is the Life Flight emergency air ambulance, which celebrated transporting its 10,000th patient in mid-1993.

The Baptist Orthopaedic Institute offers a full circle of care within a single group practice, including care for the foot and ankle, spine, shoulder, and hand, along with total joint and sports medicine services. In addition, the Institute is contributing to important research projects and various therapies in orthopaedic medicine, and provides a full range of educational opportunities.

Another unique group practice which has brought physicians and a major medical center together is the Baptist Eye Institute. It was established by a group of

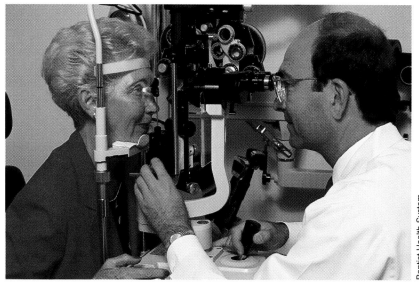

forward-thinking ophthalmologists and Baptist administrators who explored ways to provide centralized, high-quality and cost-effective outpatient eye care. In 1991, Baptist Eye Institute was established as the first comprehensive multi-specialty eye institute associated with a major medical center in the region, combined with the unique Eye Care Network, comprised of ophthalmologists and optometrists throughout the area. Eye Institute services include cataract surgery and intraocular lens implants, corneal transplants, glaucoma treatment and surgery, laser surgery, ophthalmic plastic surgery, retinal and vitreous surgery, and neuroophthalmological surgery.

The jewel in the crown of Baptist Medical Center and our community is the new $45 million, 180-bed Wolfson Children's Hospital, made possible by the outstanding support of our region's families, corporations, and national philanthropic entities. Specially designed to provide a nurturing, protective environment with every child's well-being in mind, the new hospital will serve tens of thousands of young patients — from infants to teenagers — each year. The new facility visually serves the imagination of children while, at the same time, physical and spiritual healing take place. Medical equipment and instruments fit the child. It is a place for and about children, as evidenced by its

architecture, where form and function meet the special needs of children's health care. As the only children's hospital between Orlando and Atlanta, Wolfson Children's Hospital serves the healthcare needs of our children today to prepare them for the challenges of tomorrow.

While Baptist has grown immeasurably from its modest beginnings, the people who make up Baptist Health System have never lost sight of their corporate mission: to provide high-quality heathcare services which are easily accessible and reasonably priced. Baptist holds dear certain values, those of compassion, service excellence, integrity, community involvement, stewardship of resources, and innovation. This commitment to mission is evidenced by the sincere and dedicated efforts of each member of the Baptist family — the physicians, employees and volunteers who support the continuous quality improvement effort of the System.

"We base our success on the relationships we build with people," says William C. Mason, FACHE, president and CEO of Baptist Health System. "The entire Baptist family firmly believes that it is through these relationships — nurtured by trust, medical excellence, volunteerism and philanthropy — that we are able to build the foundation of our future into the 21st century."

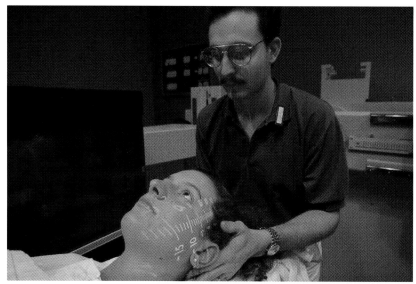

In the heart of the historic Riverside/Avondale area, St. Vincent's Health System continues its nearly 80-year legacy of providing high quality health care to the community of Jacksonville.

As a part of the Daughters of Charity National Health System, St. Vincent's Health System carries out its Mission of caring for the sick and the poor in many ways every day.

The Health System includes St. Vincent's Medical Center, a 528-bed tertiary care hospital; Riverside Hospital, a 198-bed general acute care hospital; St. Catherine Laboure' Manor, a 240-bed nursing home; and the Family Medical Care Centers with locations throughout the greater Jacksonville area.

St. Vincent's Medical Center is best known for its tradition of excellence and compassion in the fields of cardiology, oncology, emergency care and maternity. Begun in 1916 by the Daughters of Charity, St. Vincent's has grown into a thriving medical community that includes the latest state-of-the-art medical technology administered with caring and compassion.

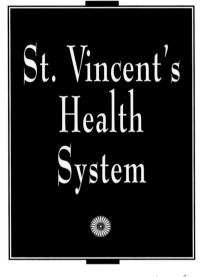

A two-track Emergency Room offers streamlined medical care for those with minor injuries or major trauma. By providing individualized tracks for each, St. Vincent's speeds service for everyone requiring emergency medical attention.

The Heart & Lung Institute at St. Vincent's is a recognized leader in cardiac care and research in Jacksonville. Cutting edge technology is practiced here, including new cardiac procedures unavailable anywhere else in the city. Research into the complicated and sometimes mysterious diseases of the heart and the lungs also is conducted at St. Vincent's, including an important nationally-funded study on increased lung cancer rates in Duval County. The Heart & Lung Institute educates and informs through such services as the Moody Gallery, an interactive gallery that explains the workings of the heart and lungs. Seminars, classes and support groups are a regular part of St. Vincent's educational efforts to reduce heart and lung disease.

Max. D. Moody Gallery (St. Vincent's Health System)

The Maternity Suites at St. Vincent's offer a one-of-a-kind birthing experience in Jacksonville. Here, in beautifully-decorated rooms, women labor, deliver and recover all in the same room. But don't be fooled by the lavish appearance and home-like furnishings — the Maternity Suites each contain the latest in medical technology all neatly tucked away behind curtains and doors, but ready at a moment's notice.

St. Vincent's dedication to medical excellence includes a complete cancer care center with diagnostic, treatment, education and research facilities all on campus. Diagnostic services include CAT scans, Magnetic Resonance Imaging (MRI) and ultrasound. Treatment services include chemotherapy, brachytherapy and radiation therapy. Physicians skilled in the diagnosis and treatment of cancer also participate in national studies to determine the effectiveness of new medications and treatments for cancer. One such study is the nationwide study of tamoxifen, a drug being evaluated for its ability to prevent breast cancer. Women at high risk here in Jacksonville are participating in this very important Breast Cancer Prevention Trial. St. Vincent's has established the Breast Cancer Center and the Lung Cancer Center to improve coordination of diagnosis and treatment for these services for patients and physicians.

Riverside Hospital is one of the oldest health care facilities in Jacksonville and today maintains a reputation for personalized and caring service. Specializing in orthopedics and psychiatric care, Riverside Hospital also provides general medical care for most specialties, emergency care and services for seniors.

The Foot Clinic at Riverside Hospital offers complete foot care for everyone, including senior citizens and diabetics. Offered regularly each week, the Foot Clinic is staffed by highly qualified podiatrists who can diagnose and treat foot ailments.

Riverside Hospital also offers a unique psychiatric program that combines medicine and psychiatry to meet all the needs of our patients. The psychiatric program helps many patients who have both psychological and medical problems. Riverside also offers a Christian Psychiatric program which is designed to combine psychiatric care with the spiritual guidance of the patient's own religious organization.

The Riverside Clinic, which first established the hospital early in this century, is a multi-specialty group of physicians located next to Riverside Hospital. Representing all primary care areas and most specialties, Riverside Clinic also offers diagnostic capabilities such as x-ray and ultrasound.

St. Catherine Laboure' Manor is conveniently located on St. Vincent's campus and adjacent to the picturesque St. Johns River. As home to more than

Riverside Hospital

200 residents, St. Catherine offers full-time nursing and therapeutic care to the elderly and others who need long-term care.

St. Catherine opened its beautiful and spacious new facility in late 1992. A specialized unit cares for those with memory impairment such as Alzheimer's Disease. St. Catherine includes comfortable rooms with home-like touches, lovely gardens and getaway spots, a large and inviting dining room, a beauty/barber shop, dental office, chapel and library.

Residents and family members work closely with the staff at St. Catherine to develop personalized care plans that are specific to the needs of each resident. Family members are encouraged to participate in the many programs and activities offered at St. Catherine LaBoure' Manor.

St. Vincent's Family Medical Care Centers are convenient physician offices located throughout the

St Catherine LaBoure Manor

greater Jacksonville area. These offices are staffed by skilled and caring Family Practice and Internal Medicine physicians who work closely with St. Vincent's Health System to maintain the good health of their patients. Most insurance plans are accepted by the Family Medical Care Centers and same-day appointments usually are available.

As Jacksonville's largest health care system, St. Vincent's Health System reaches out in dozens of ways to improve and maintain the wellness of our neighbors. Through Mobile Mammography, ambulance services, our Mobile Health Van, the Wellness Center, the Mandarin School of Good Health and dozens of other programs and services, St. Vincent's continues its decades-old commitment to the good health of Jacksonville. Crafted by the Daughters of Charity in 1916, our Mission remains:

"To witness to the healing ministry of Christ by providing quality health services in an atmosphere that fosters respect and compassion."

SUMC Lobby

Situated on 240 wooded acres just three miles from the Atlantic Ocean, Mayo Clinic Jacksonville was Mayo's first extension outside Rochester, Minnesota. The move was an effort to better serve a population quickly shifting toward the Sun Belt.

Mayo's integrated team approach provides diagnosis, treatment and surgery. At Mayo, patient care is supported by programs in medical education and research. Physicians representing more than 40 different specialties work together under one roof to enhance and streamline patient care.

Since opening in 1986, Mayo Clinic Jacksonville has seen rapid growth, more than doubling the size of its main facility, the Davis Building, to eight stories. The clinic's $15.5 million Birdsall Medical Research Building, completed in August 1993, is inspiring hope for treating Alzheimer's disease and other brain-related disorders. Mayo's expansion continues, with construction underway for an ambulatory surgery and radiation oncology facility.

A major local employer, Mayo Clinic Jacksonville has 153 physicians and a support staff of more than 1,000. The staff stays in close contact with Mayo's other sites in Rochester, Minnesota, and Scottsdale, Arizona, through an ultramodern satellite video communications system. This "telemedicine" system allows patients in Jacksonville to benefit from consultations with Mayo specialists at any location, as needed.

Mayo Clinic Jacksonville has provided care to more than 150,000 patients from all 50 states and about 75 countries. Patients with medical problems that are difficult to diagnose and treat benefit from Mayo's integrated system of care. Although Mayo works with doctors from throughout the Southeast, a physician referral is not necessary. Special services include computer-assisted stereotactic neurosurgery, a Nicotine Dependence Center, an Executive Health

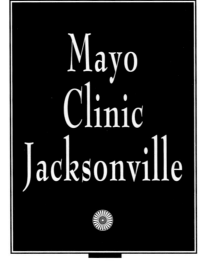

Program and a Sleep Disorders Center. The Mayo Family Medicine Center offers primary care to area residents. Patients who need hospitalization are admitted to nearby St. Luke's Hospital, which affiliated with Mayo in 1987.

Through its partnership with Alimacani Elementary School and Raines High School, Mayo works to improve science and math programs for local students. Mayo's Health Careers Scholarship Program provides financial assistance and recognition to area high school seniors pursuing careers in healthcare.

Mayo Clinic Jacksonville's plans include becoming a national and international medical destination, while continuing a strong commitment to its North Florida location. As a convenient, efficient and comprehensive medical complex, it will carry the Mayo tradition of excellence into the 21st century.

Mayo Clinic Jacksonville

Called "The Miracle on Eighth Street" by many, including hospital President Marcus E. Drewa, Methodist Medical Center has undergone a dramatic transformation since it was founded in 1967.

The institution's growth during the past three decades includes the construction of twin medical/professional towers, the expansion of an adjacent four-block area including a state-of-the-art hospital complex, parking area and professional building; the development of property on the city's northside to provide long-term skilled nursing care; and the refurbishing of the original hospital building to provide a residential setting for persons with AIDS — St. John's Place.

Methodist Medical Center, a 244-bed, not-for-profit medical center, has undergone many service changes as well over the years to complement and fully utilize the new facilities provided by the physical growth. Many services that are duplicated by other hospitals were replaced by services unmatched in this part of the state.

The establishment of the Jacksonville Transplant Center in 1989 put Methodist Medical Center in the forefront of transplant services in Jacksonville and the surrounding communities. The center's medical team provides kidney transplants for those with end-stage renal disease. Over the past year transplants have been possible for many who otherwise would have had to travel to other cities.

The Laboratory for Transportation and Cellular Immunology is a support service for the transplant center. Tissue typing as well as specialized testing can be processed to prevent area hospitals from having to send samples out of the city for testing.

The Jacksonville Marrow Donor Registry was established in 1988 to provide a local link to the national chain for providing volunteer bone marrow donors. The program has gained the support of various community members including the Fraternal Order of Police, AT&T American Transtech and CSX Transportation.

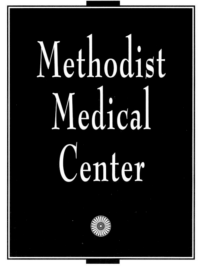

Methodist Medical Center, "The Miracle on Eighth Street," has brought unmatched medical services to Jacksonville during its nearly 30 years as a community member.

Photo by Jimmy Shover

Photo by Jimmy Shover

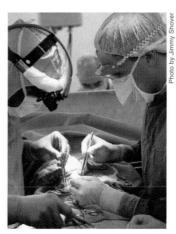

The Jacksonville Transplant Center provides the area's only resource for solid organ transplantation.

To assist employees in providing quality care and a safe work environment for their employees, EmployMed Occupational Health Services was established. EmployMed delivers health screenings, physicals, on-site drug screening as well as many other services from three locations as well as Methodist's emergency room.

The Diabetes Treatment Center at Methodist Medical Center is the most comprehensive program in the city for diabetes care, management, education and support. Recognized by the American Diabetes Association for its excellence, the program provides both inpatient and outpatient services.

Methodist Pathway Center for Chemical Dependency Treatment is the only dedicated unit for alcohol and drug rehabilitation with a full-service medical center back-up. Pathway provides comprehensive, individually-tailored plans that include care for the family of the chemically dependent person.

Florida's First Comprehensive Hospice program, Methodist Hospice, is a model program for many. A dedicated unit for pain control and respite care is the unique feature that sets Methodist Hospice apart from others. A full staff of nurses, doctors, volunteers, aides, social workers, chaplains and administration, as well as a dedicated board of directors adds a special kind of caring that is delivered to those with life-limiting illness and their family members. The medical directors still make housecalls when needed.

Methodist Medical Center also offers ABC Home Health Services, long-term nursing center care, the Methodist Education Center and many other general acute-care services.

The Methodist Medical Center Board of Directors have announced future expansion programs which will certainly increase Methodist's ability to provide the highest quality medical care in all areas, especially those unique to Methodist. Construction on a walkway over the Eighth Street intersection, a radiation/oncology center and a third 10-story professional tower are planned for the remainder of the 90s.

Customer focused . . . worthy of trust . . . respect for each other . . . winning. These are the Core Values of the company with the strength of the Rock of Gibraltar: The Prudential. The Prudential Core Values have been embraced as part of the company's culture — crossing all levels and affiliated organizations.

In Jacksonville, The Prudential Health Care System has differentiated itself within the community by advancing the Core Values and forming partnerships with health care providers who share the same vision to develop a unique and integrated health care delivery system for the benefit of the community.

Prudential has found that one of the key ingredients to a succcessful managed care plan is the primary care physician who manages and coordinates each patient's health care needs. Through its partnership with the Jacksonville Health Care Group (JHCG), the largest primary care physician group in Northeast Florida, Prudential provides its members with access to more than 35 physicians specializing in family practice, internal medicine, and pediatrics. JHCG provides a full complement of health care services to Prudential's managed care members in seven health centers located in the heart of Jacksonville's neighborhoods: Mandarin, Orange Park, Westside, Northside, Arlington, and the Southside. The seventh location is employer-based and housed in a Southside office park, the first of its kind in Jacksonville. Each health center is designed with patient convenience and satisfaction in mind with most services available under one roof, including an on-site pharmacy, full service lab, minor surgical services and a radiology department. Further, there is a full complement of individual physicians who participate in the the Prudential managed care plans, practicing in their own offices and located throughout the five counties of Northeast Florida.

Another key partnership exists between Prudential and Baptist Medical Center/ Baptist Medical Center-*Beaches*. Baptist provides most hospital services for Prudential members in Duval County and is clearly recognized in the community as a leading hospital in Northeast Florida.

The third partnership is with Southeast Pharmacy Consultants, Inc. (SPC), which operates the on-site

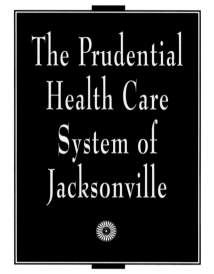

The Prudential Health Care System of Jacksonville

pharmacies located conveniently within the PruCare health centers. SPC's mission is to coordinate the effective use and management of prescription drugs to affect the best possible patient outcomes.

An approach to managed care benefits which The Prudential Health Care System of Jacksonville has found to be attractive to employers is the "dual option" that combines a health maintenance organization (PruCare® HMO) plan and a point-of-service (PruCare Plus ®) plan into one "package." The next generation of managed care products will carry The Prudential Health Care System into the managed Medicare and Medicaid markets and possibly into the Worker's Compensation arena.

The Group Department, the business unit which provides health insurance products to the employer community, entered the managed care business with its first HMO in Houston, Texas, in 1975 and in Jacksonville in 1984. From that first year they have achieved many milestones of success — licensure and Federal Qualification were granted in 1984; accreditation by the National Committee for Quality Assurance in 1992; and were ranked the #1 HMO in Jacksonville for three years in a row based on financial stability, ability to control costs, and the quality of the provider network. The future looks equally as bright. The strength and long-term vision of The Prudential combined with the quality and expertise of its chosen partners make for a winning team in Jacksonville. At The Prudential Health Care System of Jacksonville, these go beyond mere words — they're a responsibility . . . an obligation . . . a commitment.

ACKNOWLEDGMENTS

Each of the following corporate profile companies made a valuable contribution to this project. Longstreet Press gratefully acknowledges their participation.

Baita International Inc.
BancBoston Mortgage Corporation
Baptist Health System Inc.
Barnett Bank of Jacksonville, N.A.
Carter
Continental Cablevision of Jacksonville
CSX Transportation
First Union National Bank of Florida
Gate Petroleum Company
Homewood Suites Jacksonville
Intermedia Communications of Florida Inc.
Jacksonville Chamber of Commerce
City of Jacksonville
KPMG Peat Marwick
Law Engineering
Marriott at Sawgrass Resort
Mayo Clinic Jacksonville
Memorial Medical Center of Jacksonville
Methodist Medical Center
Peoples Gas System
Prudential Health Care System of Jacksonville
Prudential Insurance and Financial Services
St. Luke's Hospital
St. Vincent's Health System
Saxelbye Architects, Inc.
Scott-McRae Group
Southern Bell
Sprint/United Telephone-Florida
University Club
University Medical Center
Vistakon
Watson Realty Corp. REALTORS
White Line Trucking Inc.

This book was published in cooperation with the Jacksonville Chamber of Commerce and would not have been possible without the support of its members. Longstreet is especially grateful to the following individuals for their commitment and for their continued assistance.

Walter M. Lee, III
Susan L. Milhoan

We would also like to thank the following individuals who contributed in a variety of ways to the quality of *Jacksonville: Center for Enterprise Excellence on Florida's First Coast.*

Bert Charest
Marvin Edwards
Robert Johnson
Beverly Morgan
Stephen Tanner
Louis Woods

The following publications and organizations provided excellent sources for the text:

Wood, Wayne. *Jacksonville's Architectural Heritage: Landmarks for the Future.* University of North Florida Press, 1989.

Crooks, James B. Jacksonville *After the Fire, 1901-1919: A New South City.* University of North Florida Press, 1989.

Myers, Ronald & Ewel, John. *Ecosystems of Florida.* University of Central Florida Press, 1990.

The Florida Times-Union
Jacksonville Community Council Inc.
The Jacksonville Historical Society
The Jacksonville Public Library

PHOTOGRAPHY CAPTIONS

Index